RED ALERT!

RED ALERT!

Saving the Planet with Indigenous Knowledge

Daniel R. Wildcat

FULCRUM

Wheat Ridge, Colorado

Library of Congress Cataloging-in-Publication Data

Wildcat, Daniel R.
  Red alert! : saving the planet with indigenous knowledge / Daniel R. Wildcat.
     p. cm.
  Includes bibliographical references.
  ISBN 978-1-55591-637-4 (pbk.)
  1. Human ecology. 2. Indigenous peoples--Ecology. 3. Traditional ecological knowledge. I. Title.
  GF41.W53 2009
  304.2--dc22
                              2009019705

Printed in the United States
0 9 8 7 6 5 4 3

Design by Jack Lenzo
Cover image: *Inheriting the Legacy* by Bunky Echo-Hawk

Fulcrum Publishing
3970 Youngfield Street
Wheat Ridge, Colorado 80033
800-992-2908 • 303-277-1623
fulcrumbooks.com

The Spiritual Person of the universe, God, if you will, grant us wisdom as we talk about issues that are so very important to us.

— Angayuqaq Oscar Kawagley,
Yupiaq elder and scholar

CONTENTS

INTRODUCTION

The Climate Is Changing—
and, Well, It Should

Would it not be more accurate to say that the North American wants to use reality rather than to know it? In some matters—death, for example—he not only has no desire to understand it, he obviously avoids the very idea.

—Octavio Paz, *The Labyrinth of Solitude*

I get angry when I think about global warming, or global burning, as I prefer to designate this world phenomenon, the reasons for which will become quite clear in chapter 6. I get angry because I know the history of involuntary removals and relocations indigenous peoples throughout the United States and around the world have endured. So when nearly a decade ago I began hearing the reports of what was beginning to manifest itself on the landscapes and seascapes of the circumpolar arctic and banks of the Yukon River in Alaska, I got angry. Angry because I thought, *Here we go again—another removal of indigenous peoples.*

THREE REMOVALS, NOW A FOURTH

Contrary to what is found in US history books, many of us encountered in our peoples' histories at least three removal attempts. Many of us have trails-of-tears stories. From one shore to the other on this continent, there are many stories of removal from indigenous homelands, stories beyond the most well-known removal of the so-called civilized tribes of the southeastern United States to Oklahoma in 1838. For many, these removals were deadly. For survivors, who understood their tribal identities as peoples as emergent from their homelands, these removals were devastating.

The stubborn resilience of our ancestors was again sorely tested during a second displacement: the removal of our children from our homes and families to off-reservation boarding schools. These removals were done by "friends" of Indians who wanted to solve the "Indian problem" with the classic liberal solution to all social problems: education. But, in this case, that meant education in off-reservation boarding schools. One of the surest methods for destroying a people, their families, communities, and culture is to take their children away. This social removal, which continued well into the twentieth century, still has lasting and dysfunctional consequences for the health and wellness of American Indians and Alaska Natives. In the present era, so much talk is directed toward nation-building activities, yet this removal constituted nothing short of a nation-destroying effort from which indigenous peoples are still recovering.

The removal of children takes on an even more sinister air when it is understood that boarding-school education programs were premised on the necessity of stripping

Native children of all features of their unique tribal identities and cultures. Education was only one, albeit the most potent, representative of the final removal attempt waged by every social institution that American society could bring to bear on who we were as indigenous peoples. Religion, law, economy, education, and family, all of the social institutions of the late nineteenth century, were attacked as "civilization" sought to remove from our peoples our Indianness—our indigenousness. These institutions brought to bear on our peoples Captain Richard Henry Pratt's guiding principle for Indian education, as summed up at the nineteenth annual National Conference of Charities and Correction held in Denver, Colorado, in 1892: "Kill the Indian in him and save the man." This principle resulted in a policy now widely recognized as the embodiment of cultural genocide.

Despite these three removals—geographic, social, and psycho-cultural—many American Indians and Alaska Natives still have their languages, songs, ceremonies, and tribal identities. For those who faced all three removal attempts, there has been an intergenerational transmission of trauma, yet also often a tenacious resilience. The legacy of these histories is complex, even contradictory, and difficult to neatly summarize. Fortunately, a good number of American Indians and Alaska Natives have maintained thousand- and hundred-years-old relationships with specific landscapes and seascapes. The knowledges embodied in these deep spatial relationships to homelands have served indigenous peoples well when governmental policies and programs offered only suffering and sadness. In a world where increasing numbers of people live in highly manufactured landscapes of suburbs and subdivisions, the ancient deep spatial knowledges of people and place held by American Indians and Alaska Natives are crucial if humankind is to find sustainable ways to live in a life-enhancing manner.

Sadly, some of us now face another removal. Of course, this time things are different. This removal is not simply a governmental social policy imperative of the non-indigenous majority population. This relocation is mandated by a much deeper, more fundamental crisis: the way we live. Not everyone on the planet, but those of us who are immersed in or living in the interstices of modern industrial and now postindustrial societies. As ice sheets and glaciers melt, permafrost thaws, and seacoasts and riverbanks erode in the near and circumpolar arctic, peoples indigenous to these places will be forced to move, not as a result of something their Native lifeways produced, but because the most technologically advanced societies on the planet have built their modern lifestyles on a carbon energy foundation that has several problematic consequences and one deadly consequence: the emission of carbon dioxide.

In a physical sense this reality is what will probably be known, as writer Bill McKibben pointed out nearly fifteen years ago in *The New York Times Magazine*, as the most fundamental chemistry lesson for the twenty-first century: burning one gallon of gasoline in your automobile inevitably results in the placement of five and a half pounds of carbon dioxide, the major culprit in global burning, into the atmosphere. Keep in mind that transportation only accounts for about 33 percent of our carbon footprint in the United States, while residential and commercial buildings account for 39 percent, with the balance of our carbon dioxide produced by industrial activities, and one can see that addressing our dependence on fossil-fueled cars and trucks is only the tip of the proverbial iceberg, and a melting one at that, but one that must be addressed immediately. For societies with cultures entrenched in carbon-based energy technologies, the magnitude of the changes that need to be made in how we, humankind, think and live are immense. The removals resulting from our climate-burning activities will affect every nation on the planet.

A CULTURAL CLIMATE CHANGE

The most difficult changes required are not those of a physical, material, or technological character, but changes in worldviews and the generally taken-for-granted values and beliefs that are embedded in modern, Western-influenced societies. In this respect, what humankind actually requires is a climate change—a cultural climate change, a change in our thinking and actions—if we are to have any reasonable expectation that we might mitigate what increasingly appears to be a period of dramatic plant and animal extinction.

In order to deal with the array of social and ecological issues we will face across nearly every dimension of the complex life system of Mother Earth, we must begin to understand our lives as essentially *not* only about us, but about our human selves in what environmental scientists and ecologists, without the least hint of romanticism, call the web of life. The web of life, if taken seriously, implies that our human intelligence must be framed in the context of learning how to live well and sustainably as one small but powerful part of nature, as opposed to strategizing how to manage nature. In short, the atmospheric climate change we must try to avoid, or at least minimize, as a result of our climate-burning activities can only be addressed with a climate shift in our thinking and behavior: a cultural climate shift.

In order to acknowledge the complexity of this global-burning phenomenon, we should acknowledge that the way in which the effects of carbon dioxide–caused climate change manifest themselves will vary from place to place, from landscape to seascape. Some places, such as the British Isles, will likely experience much colder winters as a result of the melting Arctic ice cap, which infuses large amounts of freshwater into the salt water of the Atlantic Ocean, thereby diminishing the warming effect of the heavier salt water, which sinks, as the colder freshwater stays on the surface. In their midcontinent regions, large landmasses will experience erratic fluctuations in weather and more frequent extreme weather events of larger magnitude. If you doubt this, ask adults who have lived their entire lives in the central plains how seasons and weather events have changed in their lifetimes.

The term *climate change* accurately captures the diversity of the changes humankind will experience in different places across the planet as a result of what will hopefully be a relatively short, final era of fossil fuel–burning economies on Mother Earth. But even this term lends itself to abuse by those who either out of ignorance confuse weather with climate or, in the service of ideology, insist, "So what? The climate is always changing," with no regard for the sudden and dramatic features of this human-induced event.

Every credible scientific report released in the past four years documents that Mother Earth is undergoing climate change at a rate much faster than previous models have suggested. The recent meeting of the International Scientific Congress on Climate Change, a congress of twenty-five hundred delegates from around the world, is no exception. At the end of their March 2009 meeting, they issued a statement with six key findings. First among them was the following:

> Recent observations confirm that, given high rates of observed emissions, the worst-case IPCC [Intergovernmental Panel on Climate Change] scenario trajectories (or even worse) are being realized. For many key parameters, the climate system is already moving beyond the patterns of natural variability within which our society and economy have developed and thrived. These parameters include global mean surface temperature, sea-level rise, ocean and ice sheet dynamics, ocean acidification, and extreme climatic events. There is a significant risk that many of the trends will accelerate, leading to an increasing risk of abrupt or irreversible climatic shifts.[1]

The startling picture of our near future that is emerging from scientific assessments suggests that previous worst-case scenarios have underestimated the rate at which the climate of our Mother Earth is changing. When scientists—level-headed, objective thinkers—tell us we must act now in order to avert a global climate catastrophe, it is understandable that for many a sense of doom, an almost fatalistic paralysis, can set in based on a feeling that it is too late for humankind to do anything to address our current planetary situation.

Writing about climate change as an indigenous person, a Euchee (Yuchi) member of the Muscogee Nation, has been difficult. I have fought two responses to the dangerous situations in which many indigenous peoples now find themselves and growing numbers of non-Native people will soon find themselves: anger and a fatalistic sense of hopelessness. This is frustrating and useless, for sustained anger and despair inevitably lead to dead-ends along roads that literally and figuratively, physically and metaphysically indigenous peoples did not construct.

The anger results from yet another removal scenario for indigenous peoples who are facing catastrophic and deadly situations in which, strictly speaking, their indigenous cultures had no part. Despair and hopelessness can easily insinuate themselves in our everyday lives when knowledge seems so difficult to act upon because of our human inattentiveness to the world around us. When one recognizes how easy it is to be unaware of what is happening in those places and spaces we did not create—the environment beyond the interior spaces in which modern humankind spends the vast majority of their lives—the lack of urgency felt by the general public is understandable, but no less frustrating.

However, unlike some of my angst-ridden existentialist or postmodern friends, I see neither anger nor despair nor the ensuing frustration as fundamentally defining features of the human condition. Fortunately for me and many others, these emotions do not last long once one recognizes what is happening and decides to take action; Though a righteous indignation remains for those few who from the comfort of their isolated broadcast booths want to proclaim that the climate change resulting from global burning is a scientific hoax. US broadcast ideologues, who use our present climate situation as a vehicle for their exhortations, validate Octavio Paz's assessment that "the North American wants to use reality rather than to know it."

INDIGENOUS REALISM

Fortunately, thanks to indigenous elders like Oren Lyons, Billy Frank Jr., Albert White Hat, Angayuqaq Oscar Kawagley, and Henrietta Mann, to name but a few, I am constantly reminded that our human knowledge of reality must always be approached with humility. In North America many indigenous traditions tell us that reality is more than just facts and figures collected so that humankind might wisely use resources. Rather, to know "it"—reality— requires respect for the relationships and relatives that constitute the complex web of life. I call this indigenous realism, and it entails that we, members of humankind, accept our inalienable responsibilities as members of the planet's complex life system, as well as our inalienable rights.

In order to accept our inalienable responsibilities, we must now pay attention to what is happening in the natural world beyond the physical walls that enclose us and the alluring media windows we ironically look and listen to in order to feel connected. The cause of what some now call ecological amnesia is found in our human fascination with technology. We have created a global satellite-driven digital media world—a media culture—that quite literally isolates us from the natural environment that we participate in daily and that those of us in postindustrial societies most often participate in through construction and production proxy as a result of our insatiable appetite for consumption.

Some of us have so well-insulated ourselves from the inconvenient and uncomfortable features of the natural world, we fail to see that in the process we have isolated ourselves from the convenient, comfortable, and beautiful features of that same natural world of which we are one very small, but powerful, and now destructive part. Before progress—the idea and the people who enacted the idea—covered the globe, our ancestors lived in cultures that were emergent from the places where we lived.

THE STATUS QUO WILL NOT DO

The alert embodied in this book is at least twofold. First, to let people know the status quo is no longer good enough with respect to how humankind interacts and relates with the life system of Mother Earth. As Billy Frank Jr., member of the Nisqually Tribe and chairman of the Northwest Indian Fisheries Commission, so emphatically stated in his keynote address at the Planning for Seven Generations Conference at the University Corporation for Atmospheric Research in Boulder, Colorado, in 2008, we have to tell the truth. Frank stressed that the status quo is unacceptable: "People have to wake up—they have to wake up to this change that is happening right in front of us." He continued, saying, "The status quo idea that you don't scare people won't work either." Frank emphasized, "I think we better be scared."[2]

Frank related how on an ordinary day many people look around them and see that everything is running—the trains, our cars, albeit the traffic is slow, but the coffee at your favorite place tastes great. He stated, "We wake up, everything is working. We think everything is good—until we go to a meeting and find out everything is not good." This alert is a call for us to start paying attention, as my friend and mentor Vine Deloria Jr. said in *The World We Used to Live In*. For, like the book to which he gave that title suggests, we may well find a spiritual sustainability as well as a physical or material one.

This alert is also a wake-up to call to those always forward-looking societies that have failed to inquire into the modes of living of indigenous peoples that their histories interrupted and ultimately destroyed. The exercise is not a call to archaeology and anthropology as these disciplines have been practiced throughout much of their Western academic existence, but a challenge to replace a search for humankind's general development along a Western-inspired universal timeline with a rethinking of our diverse human cultural development as shaped by places. This awakening seems to be very real—more than a media buzz—and if so, those paying attention do not have to start from scratch. This alert calls attention to the fact that indigenous peoples possess precisely such place-shaped knowledges. We are indeed facing a climate change, and in order to effectively address this change, our cultural climate will have to change too.

An indigenous inheritance exists for humankind that takes many forms from many places and peoples regarding how humankind might reexamine lifeways that, although hardly without failures and mistakes, suggest in practical terms how we might adopt life-enhancing cultures situated in a symbiotic relationship with nature. Will this indigenous inheritance be denied and go unclaimed? I hope not, for the sake of the rich diversity of life we share this planet with and for the sake of our human selves. It is time to issue a Red Alert.

CHAPTER ONE

Pay Attention: An Indigenous Lesson Worth Thinking About

Henry Collins, a respected Ponca southern plains drummer and singer, gave me much to think about twenty-one years ago when I started teaching at Haskell Indian Junior College, now Haskell Indian Nations University. Collins took a social-problems course from me. He was very attentive in class and seldom spoke. When I asked him questions, he would take his time and always answer directly to the point. Nevertheless, I thought the situation awkward, because then, as now, I thought of Collins as an elder. How do you ask questions to an elder about sociological theories, concepts, and facts? It seems so rude and arrogant to question an elder as we do young undergraduate students without the least bit of hesitancy.

I remember at the end of the course I asked Collins if he had learned anything useful. Collins thought a while and said, "Yes, I think so, but it worries me because, as I put these new ideas up here [he pointed to his head], it seems like I have trouble remembering some songs." He continued, "It makes me think that I might not have room in my head for all of this new stuff—that if I put the new information in my head, I might lose some songs. That worries me. I don't want to lose those songs." Two decades ago, this is what Collins gave me to think about, and I have often done so.

Now, as I write about some of the indigenous insights and knowledges that reside in the landscapes and seascapes of North America situated in what we, American Indians and Alaska Natives, take to be a fundamentally spiritual cosmos, it occurs to me that many of us have filled our heads with the "new stuff." We have acquired elaborate theories, concepts, and ideas about our species, nature, cultures, and civilizations, and in the process forgotten important insights our ancestors possessed. Like Collins's concern for songs that embody tribal traditions of knowledge and knowing, I, too, worry that such knowledge is threatened. Life lessons, principles, born of experience in the world, as opposed to experiments in controlled laboratory settings or scientifically guided social experiments, seem absent today.

LIFE LESSONS BORN OF EXPERIENCE

As I think now of Collins's words, I wonder how many good songs, practices, and ceremonies about living well in this world humankind may have collectively lost because modern human societies so little value knowledges found beyond the protocols of narrowly defined scientific inquiry. This book is a call for indigenous recollection, reconstruction, and indigenous ingenuity. We cannot go back to the past. We must envision and enact a realization of beauty in the present for the future: a beauty unlike the superficial images sold in increasingly commercial consumer-driven modern and postmodern societies. As my Haudenosaunee friends constantly remind me, we have a responsibility to live respectfully for our children seven generations into the future.

The issue, as Collins put it so clearly, is not that one kind of knowledge or specific body of information is necessarily better than the other—let us say rigorous empirical science versus experiential knowledge acquired beyond the controls of classic experimental design. But rather that, as one identifies the construction of knowledge with the logic of experiment—it seems, with few exceptions—one forgets the knowledges of experience, knowledges gained through attentive living, such as singing and drumming. We need both experimental logic and analysis and experience in the world. Collins reminded me that scientific knowledge can be useful to humankind, but, in and of itself, insufficient in generating life-enhancing knowledges for humankind.

The necessary and sufficient condition for life-enhancing knowledges requires paying attention to the life surrounding us, what I call a deep spatial experiential body of knowledge complemented by scientific information and knowledge. It would be useful if humankind understood how both kinds of knowledge were constructed. Some of us may be proficient in both, but it is more likely that a good number of us are more proficient in the lab, or at least dependent on those who are and the knowledge they produce, than we are competent in experience-based life learning. Fortunately, if those at each end of this knowledge continuum can master the difficult task of communicating with the other, humankind will benefit.

In order to acquire insights into how to live well in the diverse environments of this planet, humankind needs multigenerational deep spatial knowledges as well as scientific knowledge and its application in increasingly powerful technologies. We need to recognize the importance of the exercise of logic and analysis, but never at the expense of the songs of life handed down from singer to singer and documented in the activity of singing.

Collins never took another class from me and that is okay. I know Collins continues to sing. I am glad that he retains songs somewhere in his mind and in the act of singing. We cannot each of us do everything and know everything, but we can benefit from sharing what each of us knows that the other does not. Humankind needs useful knowledges contained in lifeways. In a world where people accept the separation of knowing from doing, it is instructive to reflect on the value of knowledges retained and realized in activity itself.

PAYING ATTENTION

The environmental crises we now face were shaped to a large extent by some of humankind not knowing what they were doing. These crises and the looming global climate catastrophe can be addressed by knowing contained in doing. The examination of knowledges embodied in the lifeways of indigenous peoples offers hope. The separation of knowing and doing so widely accepted today can be addressed if we recognize that knowledge resides in our living in this world, not in controlling it. By paying attention to our human conduct and the life beyond our own in the world surrounding us—a complex dynamic system where we, humankind, are not in control—we will find humility and wisdom. For those paying attention, knowledge resides in life.

Today many humans accept the fact that knowledge is essentially a social or collective enterprise. Many indigenous knowledge systems extend the notion of knowledge construction to a cooperative activity involving the other-than-human life that surrounds us. This book suggests that planet Earth—a living being known to many indigenous peoples today as Mother Earth—is trying to tell us something in her language.

The language of the Earth, her mother tongue, is one best understood through the many dialects known by indigenous peoples around the world. Because indigenous peoples have paid attention to our Mother Earth, it is important to listen to what we can share with humankind. These knowledges are bound in unique lifeways—customs, habits, behaviors, material and symbolic features of culture emergent from the land and sea—and therefore have practical implications for those of humankind wanting to cooperatively and sustainably live with a place as opposed to at an address.

The Red Alert issued here comes from the Earth herself. What she has been telling tribal people around the world, especially those paying attention, is that she is undergoing a dramatic change, one that threatens their lifeways and those of most of humankind on the planet. The question now is who else is listening and paying attention? Superficially it appears many are. The real test will be how many people act on what they learn. This Red Alert is for those wanting to act. Those willing to examine the public and practical features of our cultures will find life-enhancing values expressed in activity, in action.

YOU WILL BE AT THE TABLE

Our elders continue to tell our young men and women they must be ready to "sit at the table" when policies, programs, and laws are developed affecting our peoples and homelands. At the University of Arizona Vine Deloria Jr. symposium of 2006, "Where Do We Go from Here? The Legacies of Vine Deloria Jr.," Billy Frank Jr., the legendary leader of the Northwest Indian Fisheries Commission, passionately summed up where the indigenous peoples of North America are now headed. Using the twenty tribes in Washington State as an example, he stated:

> You will be co-managers with the state of Washington. You will write your own regulations...You will have your own judicial system. You will have an infrastructure that makes that happen. You are going to go to Congress and Congress will send money to every one of the tribes to build their infrastructure—to be co-managers with the state of Washington. You will have your own science, legal system, policy, and everything. So today we sit like that. We sit on that on the infrastructure of our tribes. We sit on the US international treaty commission in Canada. We sit on the body managing two hundred miles of the ocean off the [Pacific] coast—from Mexico to Alaska.

Speaking of the Magnuson-Stevens Fishery Conservation and Management Act, Frank emphasized the role the twenty American Indian tribes now play in the co-management of a two-hundred-mile zone extending into the Pacific Ocean from Mexico to Alaska:

You [the twenty tribes] will be at the table. And that is where we want to be. We want to be there when decisions are made about our life. We want to be at that table. We are capable of sitting at that table today with the federal government, with any government in the United States, to argue our case or negotiate or sit down and do it. And that is where we want to be.[1]

As we prepare to face the challenge of climate change, we not only want a seat at the table, we want to participate in discussions about research, sustainable economies and the energy to fuel them, and environmental adaptation. We want to be involved in designing research.

All of this will result in the necessity for difficult discussions on several fronts. First, historical—human and ecological—reality will inevitably present itself when the necessity for concessions is discussed. Second, the way in which issues are defined will pose a difficult challenge for scientists, policy makers, and entrepreneurs. Finally, a necessary radical reframing of environmental justice issues will have to occur if humankind is to substantially mitigate the consequences of our behavior already set in motion.

Climate change will force humankind to reexamine our comfortable notions of world history, especially the way in which modern humankind so easily distinguishes human history from what is broadly called natural history. In part, this formulation results from the fact that with the exception of violent catastrophic natural phenomena, which operate independent of our immediate human influence, human history moves rapidly when compared to the histories of mountains, oceans, and rivers. Indeed, we do seem to make things happen relatively quickly when addressing our own affairs. The reality of global climate change will certainly challenge this comfortable human-versus-nature distinction.

A RED ALERT OF HOPE

Hopefulness resides with the peoples who continue to find their identities emerge out of what I call a nature-culture nexus, a symbiotic relationship that recognizes the fundamental connectedness and relatedness of human communities and societies to the natural environment and the other-than-human relatives they interact with daily. Just as importantly, hopefulness resides with those who are willing to imaginatively reconstitute lifeways emergent from the nature-culture nexus. Over the last five centuries, some of humankind brought tremendous change to life on the planet, and the change seems essentially guided by an allegedly objective mechanical worldview that envisioned the noblest human activity as the control of nature (the machine) and the forces of nature. We now find that the complex life of Mother Earth demonstrates that such a view is naive and dangerous, for we are situated, in spite of however much we would like to think otherwise, inside, as but one part, of the life system of planet Earth.

Those expecting to find reassuring romantic reveries about noble savages living close to nature should turn elsewhere for their reading pleasure. There are no tribal secrets or ceremonies contained in these pages. There are more than enough faux-shaman reveries available on bookstore shelves to falsely and fictitiously meet those readers' very real emotional needs. However, those—Native and non-Native alike—wanting to explore practical and useful features of indigenous worldviews and knowledges should read this book.

Humankind does not stand above or outside of Earth's life system. If the planet is telling us the problem is the way much of our kind is living, it seems arrogant and unproductive to continue to want to change everything but the way we live. Yes, the world is changing, and it is time for us to pay attention—for humankind to find value in our lives as they are intrinsically related to the other-than-human life of Mother Earth. Let us do so, for like our ancestors before us, we may learn something about ourselves. We may find insights in our oldest indigenous traditions and activities. It is also likely that if we demonstrate respectful attentiveness to the world we live in today, we will find new techniques, songs, practices, and even ceremonies for life enhancement. This Red Alert expresses a desire for urgent action based on respectful attentiveness. This Red Alert is about hope, not fear.

CHAPTER TWO

The Truth Is Not Inconvenient—
It Is Deadly

For many of us immersed in industrial and postindustrial societies, the truth may indeed be inconvenient, for the time being, but for many indigenous peoples around the world, the truth of climate change is deadly. Increasingly, Native hunters of the circumpolar arctic region are losing their lives due to the unstable condition of the ice. According to Bill Erasmus, chief of the Déné Nation in northern Canada, and Patricia Cochran, Inupiat Eskimo and program chair for the indigenous program of the International Congress on Circumpolar Health, Native hunters now risk their lives every time they go out on the ice. Climate change has created a dire situation for peoples who depend on the ice for their livelihood. Nevertheless, for those living in places on the planet where the effects of global burning are less obvious, the urgency of addressing the climate change situation is difficult to convey given the self-absorbed individualistic popular culture representations of catastrophe the media sells. Many people are suspicious of catastrophe theories—cataclysms, Armageddon scenarios, societal-collapse hypotheses—and rightfully so. We have always had forecasts of imminent doom. Some people and institutions seem to thrive on catastrophe. My local Fox television affiliate is a good example of this phenomenon, as are a host of fundamentalist Christian evangelists. Consequently, it is a difficult but necessary task to explain the climate changes set in motion by taken-for-granted carbon-based energy technologies as a catastrophe without seeming like a the-sky-is-falling alarmist or without engendering hopelessness.

It is increasingly clear that we have set in motion consequences that will be damaging and deadly for much of the life we have taken for granted on our Mother Earth. Fortunately, we can take some positive, life-affirming steps to address this catastrophe by behaving respectfully and responsibly in ecological communities within which we must once again situate our lives. There is hope for ourselves and many of our other-than-human relatives if we pay attention to what the unique landscapes and seascapes and their plants and animals can still teach us. In order to respond to this Red Alert, four points must be made explicit so that what follows can be clearly distinguished from popular marketing practices, certain theological traditions, and forecasts offered by individuals with catastrophe-addicted personalities that entail an unfaltering belief in cataclysmic scenarios regardless of the facts.

HONORING AMERICAN INDIAN AND ALASKA NATIVE INSIGHTS

First, the truth is not inconvenient—it is deadly. The catastrophe humankind is currently facing is far from a purely theoretical discussion, theological debate, or psychological condition. The global-burning phenomenon pushing global climate change is for tribal nations most fundamentally a lifeway issue, one that is immediately impacting the lives of indigenous peoples around the planet—and make no mistake about it, it will soon be felt by all people across this planet. Our northern hemisphere circumpolar relatives, human and other-than-human, are experiencing the catastrophe of global burning right now. For the indigenous peoples of that region, the truth is lethal.

The recent testimony of Sheila Watt-Cloutier, Inuit activist and 2007 Nobel Peace Prize nominee, before the Inter-American Commission on Human Rights makes clear that the climate change Arctic peoples are facing threatens their cultures and lifeways:

> I am here today to talk to you about how global warming and climate change are affecting the basic survival in many vulnerable regions and, in particular, of indigenous cultures throughout the Americas.
>
> Of course, what I know best is from my own region—the Arctic, which happens to be the hardest hit by climate change. As such, many of the impacts that I will refer to will come from my own homelands. However, you can consider similar impacts on most indigenous peoples who remain integrated with their ecosystems. Inuit and other indigenous peoples continue to be an integral part, and not separate, from the ecosystems in which we live. Climate change brings into question the basic survival of indigenous people and indigenous cultures throughout the Americas.[1]

Numerous scientific organizations and many environmental writers like Wendell Berry, Bill McKibben, Kirkpatrick Sale, Barry Lopez, James Howard Kunstler, and Elizabeth Kolbert, to name a few of the best, have done a good job documenting the situation humankind has brought about on the planet. However, serious consideration, with the exception of Sale, has not been given to indigenous ways of knowing and wisdom that, as Vine Deloria Jr. formulated, still reside in the powers and places that produce our unique human personalities and collectively our cultures. Before we focus exclusively on looking for new technological solutions—and there will certainly be some—we should look at indigenous tribal knowledges for insights into how humankind might not merely survive this global crisis, but thrive in indigenously inspired cultures of life enhancement.

Second, this Red Alert is a continuation of long-standing Native American and Alaska Native traditions of issuing calls for action. These warnings—not preachings—are a call to pay attention to what is happening in the world around us and how events are affecting our human lives and the lives of our other-than-human relatives. Nearly two centuries ago, in 1811, Tecumseh issued an early indigenous Red Alert in a speech to the Choctaws and Chickasaws that invoked a metaphor that clearly resonates today:

> Where today is the Pequod? Where [are] the Narran-gansetts, the Mohawks, Pocanokets, and many other once powerful tribes of our race? They have vanished before the avarice and oppression of the white man, as snow before a summer sun...Look abroad over

their once beautiful country, and what see you now? Naught but the ravages of the pale face destroyees meet our eyes. So it will be with you Choctaws and Chickasaws! Soon your mighty forest trees, under the shade of whose wide spreading branches you have played in infancy, sported in boyhood, and now rest your wearied limbs after the fatigue of the chase, will be cut down to fence in the land which the white intruders dare call their own. Soon their broad roads will pass over the grave of your fathers, and the place of their rest will be blotted out forever.[2]

Tecumseh's warning was firmly grounded, literally and figuratively, in his experience.

Today we know the issue is not a question of race, but an issue of culture. We have seen and are currently witnessing cultures vanishing "as snow before a summer sun," and many indigenous cultures continue to be threatened. Fortunately, although much has been taken from us, many indigenous peoples have not vanished as Tecumseh and, later, noted photographer Edward S. Curtis feared. Tecumseh was correct to encourage his southern neighbors to look at the lands around them, for now, like then, we can no longer afford the inattentiveness that fosters ignorance regarding the world we live in.

Since the arrival of Europeans to our American Indian and Alaska Native homelands, many of our leaders have issued alerts based on their firsthand experiences. Many recognized that changes in our lands foreshadowed destructive changes in our lifeways. Blue Jacket, Little Turtle, Tecumseh, Ten Bears, Crazy Horse, Satanta, Seattle,

Luther Standing Bear, Black Elk, Frank Fools Crow, Melvin Thom, Joe DeLaCruz, Bob Thomas, Thomas Banyacya, Vine Deloria Jr., Henrietta Mann, John Mohawk, Oren Lyons, Billy Frank Jr., and Winona LaDuke have sounded Red Alerts that warned of what the "civilized" society and government of the United States was doing to the environments of our First Nations lands. The Red Alert here offered is consistent with their warnings and builds on an insight all these leaders embraced: our tribal lifeways are rich in values and useful knowledge.

Third, to respond to this Red Alert, we must situate our thinking and acting to the environments we did not design and build—those spaces and places beyond the walls of our human-designed interiors, computer screens, and the numerous electronic, digital, and satellite-fed media devices that increasingly form the environments we inhabit. As modern industrial civilizations developed, so, too, has a major error, possibly a fatal one. Humankind immersed in industrial and postindustrial societies tend to look at themselves, or more accurately, look *through* their human creations in order to see the world. Not surprisingly, our view of the world has been distorted. What we see is not the world, but our own images with the aid of powerful information and imaging technologies that we mistake for the world beyond ourselves.

Information technologies are important, powerful, and useful tools in our representation of the big picture of the planet's biosphere—a picture in which we are now important figures. However, as the most recent report of the Intergovernmental Panel on Climate Change makes clear, the people on the ground are experiencing changes faster than scientists can analyze and report them. The benefit of listening to what indigenous people can tell us today is twofold: first, their long-term relationships with particular landscapes and ecological systems make their observations very useful, for their longitudinal time frame "study" is not five or ten years, but often seven or more generations. Most importantly, their interaction involves what ought to be described as a deep spatial relationship to the land—an interaction embodying a sacred relationship.

In order to live well and fruitfully on this planet, humankind must sense the sacred in an experiential world beyond the human-created environments, information, and images that currently surround us. Finding ways to once again value experiential learning in the world seems the best antidote to an ideological abstraction that promotes an impoverished form of experience. The incredible technologies on which we rely so heavily have latent consequences we can recognize if we are paying attention—not the least of these is a growing insulation of our everyday lives from the living planet that sustains us.

The impoverishment of experience may be difficult to explain to those entranced in a media-driven world where we think nature is something we can only find within the boundaries of nature preserves, wilderness areas, and national parks far removed from the nature that exists right outside our doors and beyond the monitors and screens we ironically look at in order to feel "connected." It is very easy to take for granted the living Earth system of which we humans are but one small part when it is alleged throughout media-driven consumer societies that we can live so comfortably and conveniently without paying attention. Although our own lives depend on a complex web of life, it is hard for humans to respect relationships and responsibly reciprocate in this web when so many of us take it for granted and seldom directly experience it.

It is natural for humankind to develop technologies. But in the mistaken war with nature that much of humankind seems to have joined, we have forgotten that technology itself was until very recently in our human history emergent from the landscapes and ecosystems where we resided. A large part of the problem humankind now faces resides in the fact that we have lived, to a large extent, without paying attention to the world beyond the centrally cooled and heated interiors where most will read these pages. This alert calls attention to the fact that indigenous knowledges can contribute substantially to improving Mother Earth's situation.

Consequently, the fourth point is hopeful, for this Red Alert recognizes the resilience of Mother Earth and the peoples whose lives are deeply related to her landscapes and seascapes. A reasonable indigenous principle for technology development born of these deep relationships, one recognized today in appropriate technology and sustainability circles, is that technology ought to fit the natural landscape where it will be situated, or better yet, emerge from the environment itself with our help. Only naive thinkers would suggest this means going back to live exactly as our ancestors did. What this natural fitting of technology does suggest is that insights can be gained by carefully looking at the technological insights people possessed when their cultures and especially technologies were part of a symbiotic interaction in the nature-culture nexus.

The growing recognition that indigenous knowledges are emergent from the nature-culture nexus gives these knowledges a characteristic that may, in a deep sense, represent their greatest value: holistic or complex integrative thinking. They promote problem solving and action outside the dualisms and dichotomies that so typify the Western worldview—for example, material versus spiritual, science versus religion, objective versus subjective, nature versus culture, and so on. With respect to this last dichotomy, indigenous knowledges require humankind to acknowledge that until very recently, cultural diversity and biological diversity have been inextricably linked in the nature-culture nexus.

As Watt-Cloutier's testimony made clear, there are still peoples who create their cultures and identities from the unique places they call home. The climate change events we face have been brought about by a dangerous and deadly separation of culture, especially technology, from nature. Have we reached a place and time on this planet where we can overcome some of the miseducative features of the dominant Western-influenced culture exported around the planet and consider restoration of some sound indigenous wisdom? I hope so.

Culture must not be primarily conceived as something humans use to control, mediate, and reengineer nature to fit our human-scale notion of life on this planet. Rather, culture should be understood as expressions of how humans integrate their lives into the landscapes and ecosystems of the Earth's biosphere. The good news is that indigenous people today can help humankind address this. As Vine Deloria Jr. suggested nearly four decades ago, it may now be time for indigenous peoples to talk while the settlers and colonizers listen.

INDIGENOUS PEOPLES:
A WORKING DEFINITION

Indigenous peoples, as the term is used here, refers to peoples or nations who take their tribal identities as members of the human species from the landscapes and seascapes that gave them their unique tribal cultures. This definition will make problematic the issue of what it means to be indigenous for scholars, nonscholars, indigenous, and nonindigenous persons alike. I make no excuses for ensuing debate regarding what it means to be indigenous. Indeed, I welcome what my colleagues call "difficult discussions" regarding indigenousness and what it means to be indigenous.

In the increasingly geographically mobile world humans inhabit at the beginning of what Western civilization calls the twenty-first century, fewer and fewer people have tangible lifeway relationships to the places in which they live. Humankind's diets, clothing, dwellings, and everyday lives are increasingly shaped by social forces such as corporations and marketers that attempt to transcend the unique features of the peoples and places of the planet. This description includes many American Indians and increasingly Alaska Natives: these are collective names given by the European settlers who formed the US government to tribal peoples or nations now living within the political boundaries of Alaska and the contiguous forty-eight states of the United States. So what of American Indian and Alaska Native persons who have never lived in communities and cultures emergent from the places that gave them their tribal identities, cultures, and, subsequent to our Nations' treaty-making diplomacy, consecrated political rights within the US legal and political system, be it Apache, Tlingit, Passamaquoddy, Seminole, Menominee, or Lummi, to name a few of the hundreds of our nations?

I am a realist. We should count as indigenous those within the United States who can call upon what Cherokee scholar Bob Thomas identified as the taproots of people-hood: a language, a sacred history, a place or homeland, and ceremonial cycle as a part of their heritage.[3] Deloria's formulation that power plus place equals personality is also useful.[4] Thomas's and Deloria's ideas, although developed in the context of American Indian realities in North America, capture and illuminate the incredible diversity that exists among indigenous people throughout the world. Nevertheless, the truth is that today many American Indians and Alaska Natives are living in ways and places that, strictly speaking, they did not choose, but that the US government's policies and laws chose for them.

I care little for the characterization and denominations given to us by the US government or the larger society of the United States, but I recognize the importance of understanding how this (to us) foreign government has established a certain legal and political status for us within their system of laws. Our understanding is critical given the consequences our nations face within this system. A careful reading of American history will confirm that we have not been "included" into this United States so much as enclosed within it. Consequently, from where we stand, so to speak, things look much different to us, and our use of English language terms and concepts take a very different meaning. To be indigenous, as the term is used throughout this book, has little to do with formalistic or legalistic constructions. Rather, it describes persons who draw on their tribal history and culture to find ways to improve their lives and the life that surrounds them in practical ways.

OVERCOMING STEREOTYPES

The integration or reintegration of human lifeways into the environments our Mother Earth gave us will require an indigenization of worldviews for scientists, policy makers, entrepreneurs, and humankind across all our social institutions. There is reason for cautious optimism, if citizens of the United States and people living in the most industrial and industrial-supported societies on our planet are willing to discard some of their deepest intellectual and moral prejudices. Useful knowledge can be gained by listening to what indigenous people can share about their worldviews—worldviews that do not see humankind as the ultimate measure of value—and, more importantly, by examining how indigenous people act and have acted.

An honest examination of American Indian knowledges will require a critical reexamination of terms such as *tribal* and *tribalism*, *civilization* and *progress*. For with respect to the latter ideas, it appears that in those cultures committed to the world-historical projects of civilizing humankind and nature, we have actually lost much of the biological and cultural diversity that constitutes this beautiful blue-green planet. At the dawn of what in the Western calendar is reckoned to be the twenty-first century AD, those basking in a dislocated consumer culture are not so much engaged in civilizing, but rather civil-losing lifeways.

Given that the United States' current wars in Iraq and Afghanistan are often couched in terms of civilization versus tribalism, it may be hard for many Americans to imagine that something tribal or of indigenous origin could be anything other than primitive and uncivilized. And this is my point: to suggest that Native knowledge emergent from tribal lifeways can be affirming to much of what humankind says they aspire to is very difficult for most citizens of the United States to appreciate, especially when the major conflicts in which the US government is engaged are often superficially couched in the prejudicial Western dichotomy of civilized nations versus primitive tribalism. This prejudice need not be premeditated, for the very use of the terminology of *civilized nation* versus *tribal society* equals in the Western-influenced mind the dichotomy between an enlightened culture and a superstitious primitive culture to such an extent that once an enemy is identified as tribal, it becomes very hard for Americans to see anything good coming from a people understood as standing outside civilization and "progress."

There may be no more costly prejudice to life on Earth than the pseudo-evolutionary idea that tribalism is somehow categorically savage and uncivilized. Fortunately, the diverse approaches to living well on this planet are easily seen once one abandons the dramatically schizophrenic view of tribal peoples that exists in the mass media and, consequently, the minds of most of modern humankind, especially the citizens of the United States.

Overcoming the schizophrenic dichotomizing that American Indians and Alaska Natives are subjected to in the minds of modern humankind may be our greatest obstacle.

On the one hand, most Americans have in their minds the image of the modern casino-, oil-, and uranium-rich Indians living in poverty and beset by every conceivable social dysfunction known to humankind. The peculiar feature of these Indians is that they are either way too rich or poor—these Indians of the modern Euro-American imagination exist as defeated peoples. As such they have lost forever the noble culture they are understood to have once possessed. Never mind that this stereotype is so biased and self-contradictory as to be incomprehensible. The defeated modern Indian makes sense only if one understands the flip side of the defeated modern Indian stereotype.

For the defeated modern Indian is the "other" for a far more deadly stereotype: the iconic stoic noble savage that Americans love in a nearly pathological manner. I suggest pathological because this exotic Indian who comes to life in their minds in visits to powwows, cultural exhibits, and demonstrations, and now the new National Museum of the American Indian, represents the very people the government of the United States sought to destroy in its march of civilization and progress. This stereotype is every bit as crippling as the former, for it suggests that the "real" Indians are all dead. Those who love us as exotic museum and ethnographic artifacts or specimens know we are dead because this is what American history texts by and large continue to suggest through a fallacy of omission.

This stereotype is deeply revealing because it suggests that the romanticism on which it is based seems to only function in the minds of those possessed by this image once the actual peoples on which this romanticized and exoticized icon are perceived as dead. Like the defeated modern Indian stereotype—the vanished, dead Indian—the noble savage stereotype is full of contradictions also. The noble savages must have been spiritual, the modern Euro-American mind concludes, since the exotic world of the Native could not be anything like their glossy commercial and sterile manufactured world that is devoid of any phenomenal sense of the sacred.

Minus any sense of paradox, the same savage is also seen as inextricably mired in an existence marked by brutish poverty, superstition, and violence. Yet, in spite of this brutal Darwinian "struggle for existence" and Hobbesian "poor, nasty, brutish, and short" existence, we apparently possessed, according to the renderings of contemporary artists, an airbrushed "natural" beauty and Olympian strength, unrecognizable today in our highly cosmetic and overweight society.

The problem with both stereotypes is that they make it nearly impossible for people to see us as we are today. These stereotypes obscure real Natives living, working, and sometimes struggling in contemporary society to maintain unique tribal lifeways and knowledges that remain useful and may offer humankind its last best chance to develop a human maturity. Our development of responsible and respectful behaviors will provide an escape from anthropocentric immaturity that is leading many of our fellow humankind to enact forms of self-determination that are in effect self-termination.

Ahistorical and ideological prejudices have continued to preclude serious examination of indigenous knowledges that might help humankind address the current global environmental crisis. Consequently, too few people have looked circumspectly at our cultures for practical insights to facilitate not merely sustaining, but enriching life on Earth at the dawn of the twenty-first century, and tragically this includes many American Indians and Alaska Natives living in the midst of America's dominant institutions.

Even acknowledging significant cultural diffusion, many humans are awakening to the fact that throughout the world, our cultures in all their behavioral, material, symbolic, and ideational manifestations were until very recently reflections of the rich ecological diversity of places on this Earth. It is particularly telling that this awakening is occurring at a time when a critical complicating factor in the survival of our indigenous cultures is the creation of a culture, one monolithic global consumer culture that makes a sense of place—or more properly, natural land-scapes—irrelevant in its homogenizing logic. Let us hope the recognition of the inextricable coupling of cultural diversity with ecological diversity has not come too late.

We cannot save ourselves 07-07-07 style. It will take more than a worldwide media event. But we can help our-selves by participating in the life systems of this planet in more sustainable ways. We can recognize that we have rel-atives on this planet who can teach us something if we care to listen. There is too much at stake on our planet, Mother Earth, to do otherwise.

CHAPTER THREE

Sovereignty: Self-Determination or Self-Termination?

Humankind is presently immersed in a culture of self-termination. By *self-termination*, I mean that those of us living in modern industrial and postindustrial societies give every indication of attempting ecological suicide on a global scale. The uniquely calamitous feature of this culture is that we are killing ourselves by ending the lives of many of our other-than-human relatives on which our own lives depend.

The situation we currently face has been brought about in large part by the globalization of a homogenizing, one-size-fits-all culture. Tribal leaders in our indigenous nations ought to be careful in their discussions of sovereignty, self-determination, and economic development to avoid unconsciously adopting a pattern of thought that naively accepts the definitions and activities of the dominant society that surrounds them with respect to any of these ideas. If we, Native peoples, exercise self-determination to improve our lives by simply adopting the definitions, models, and activities that define the dominant culture and society surrounding us, we are likely to find ourselves enacting self-termination. This assessment is hardly hyperbole—especially since those looking closely at the life and life systems of the planet are increasingly concerned and sounding their own alerts.

THE EVIDENCE

The Species Survival Commission of the International Union for Conservation of Nature estimates the current rate of species extinction to be one hundred to one thousand times higher than the natural extinction rate. In an acknowledgment not just startling for its content but for its source, the George W. Bush administration's most recent secretary of the interior, Dirk Kempthorne, acknowledged that the polar bear may be extinct in a little less than fifty years. Worldwide, many ancient species of our planet are being threatened: giant sea turtles, orangutans, numerous species of frogs, and many others are all imperiled by our human behavior—our so-called climate warming.

The Intergovernmental Panel on Climate Change predicts that because global warming is affecting the Earth's biosphere so dramatically, there is the possibility of a total ecosystem collapse on our planet in fifty years. As these ecosystems collapse, so do the unique and sophisticated indigenous human cultures emergent from them. This issue is hardly a speculative or theoretical question for Alaska Natives today—the Earth is literally changing under their feet.

In late December of 2006 the Associated Press reported that three communities, Newtok, Shishmaref, and Kivalina, of some 183 Alaska Native villages threatened by climate warming–induced erosion are in imminent danger of collapse, literally and figuratively. Talk of relocation is difficult for peoples whose very sense of identity is defined by landscapes and seascapes that for thousands of years gave to them ways of living in a complex nature-culture nexus. For our Alaska Native brothers and sisters, climate change is far more than an "inconvenient truth": it is a catastrophic dissolution of their indigenous lifeways.

As my Yupiaq friend and colleague Angayuqaq Oscar Kawagley explained at the first annual Impact of Changing Environments on Indigenous Peoples symposium convened at Haskell Indian Nations University from June 19 to 22, 2006:

> So the cold and the culture that it made: it gave us the characteristics of our identity. It gave us the characteristics of ingenuity, adaptability, belief, and persistence. These are characteristics that were given to us by the cold. My clothing, my shelter, my food, and my technology were all engendered by the cold—and it is a very simple technology, and the technology that is best kept in the mind. Not so the modern technology that we have—I don't know what to do with the computer. I am a technological dunce and very proud of it. What if we have a major solar flare? And it knocks out the satellites, knocks out the astronauts, and knocks out the energy grids, and all of a sudden your cellular phones are useless and your computers are useless and everything else is useless. And it is my cold-based Native knowledge that will give me hope to make a life and to make a living.[1]

It would be difficult to find a more explicit practical statement of the nature-culture nexus than Kawagley's.

It was only several years ago that scientists at Lawrence Livermore National Laboratories, using a very modest model with simple assumptions, conservatively predicted that if we continue to use up the Earth's fossil fuels without dramatic reductions in carbon dioxide emissions, the ice cap in the northern hemisphere will completely disappear by 2150 and by 2300 the sea level will rise twenty-three feet. Large sections of nearly all major coastal cities in the world will be underwater, and many much sooner than 2300.

With the aid of remote sensing technologies, scientists have now confirmed that a forty-one-square-mile piece of ice, the Ayles Ice Shelf, broke free of Ellesmere Island in the Canadian Arctic during the late summer of 2005. More recently, National Oceanic and Atmospheric Administration scientists James E. Overland and Muyin Wang published their latest research in the *Geophysical Research Letters* of the American Geophysical Union showing that Arctic regional sea ice will decline by 40 percent before 2050. The Overland and Wang research ought to get everyone's attention. The forecasts for our future are getting more ominous with each passing day.

Mark Serreze, an Arctic specialist at the National Snow and Ice Data Center in Boulder, Colorado, suggests the Arctic sea ice melt has accelerated so much since 2002 (the period used as the baseline for projections by Overland and Wang was 1979 to 1999) that it is possible for the ice to completely disappear by 2030. Serreze's assessment is confirmed by scientists at the Alfred Wegener Institute for Polar and Marine Research in Bremerhaven, Germany, who have reported that large areas of sea ice have thinned by 50 percent since 2001 to the thickness of one meter. Such data is crucial, but indigenous peoples of the circumpolar arctic can tell anyone who asks them in very pragmatic terms how all hell, or at least its heat, is breaking loose in the Arctic.

Unfortunately, people can hear of these alarming developments and even watch them on the nightly news and go on about their business, thinking that such tragic developments will have little consequence to their lives in the middle of North America. This is precisely the problem: they are dead wrong. Drought, extreme weather events, and visible changes in the seasons, as we expect them to unfold, will have dramatic consequences on nearly all features of our everyday lives. Home heating and cooling, groceries, transportation, and, probably most notably in the great American West, across the Great Plains to the Rocky Mountains and to the West Coast of the United States, water will seize everyone's attention.

For the last decade the complex interactions between the diminished rainfall and numerous environmental conditions have been documented and studied by scientists and lived by the Diné people of the Four Corners region of the Southwest. In 2005 geoscientist Jacob Sewall published in the journal *Earth Interactions* the results of two computer models he ran that suggested a 30 percent decline in annual rainfall in the Southwest and an almost 40 percent decline in the Northwest. His models only confirm what US Geological Survey (USGS) scientist Margaret Hiza Redsteer reports from the field and, more importantly, what any Diné person living on the Navajo Reservation can report: the drought is already here and well underway. The USGS Navajo Nations Studies Project, led by Hiza, is now documenting the movement of sand dunes as the drought persists and researching how the drought affects the timing, type, and intensity of meteorological events as well as the landscapes of the Navajo Reservation.

A UNIQUE GLOBAL CATASTROPHE

Change happens all the time, sometimes within hours, as in the case of weather-related events and natural disasters such as tornadoes, hurricanes, floods, and mudslides. There have been earlier global catastrophes, most notably extinctions. But what makes the global catastrophe underway so unique is threefold in nature.

First, the global climate changes underway are the result of human behavior. The visible changes those with long-standing relationships to environments (including a good number of rural folks who have not been forced off their farms) can now see are the product of how a large number of us live and, apparently, given the advertisements that now circulate the globe, how some of us hope the rest of humanity will want to live. The idea that civilization, identifiable with the domination of nature, or, to be more precise, the acceptance that civilization such as it has developed through human history, especially in the last two centuries, can exist symbiotically with the rest of nature, with some minor technological tweaking, is the primary catalyst for the ensuing catastrophe we will face.

Second, while humans have created catastrophes of political, economic, and moral character throughout our

history, the change underway is radical in the sense that it marks the first known event of geologic change on a global scale caused by human activity. We are clearly witnessing changes that are geologic in character—for example, melting ice sheets, eroding and disappearing coastlines, and changes to the Earth's surface geology. By describing these events as global in scale, I mean that the changes our behavior is bringing about are on an order of magnitude similar to what we have seen in earlier planetwide extinction events on Earth.

Finally, the dramatic environmental changes underway, although geologic in character, are moving at rates of change that are very much on a human scale. Geologists, more than any other scientists, are inclined to follow Aldo Leopold's admonition to "think like a mountain," at least with respect to time, and for good reason: the dramatic Earth-system changes they study often occur over tens and hundreds of thousands of years, even millions of years. The change scenarios for climate, land, air, water, and living beings (environments and ecosystems) scientists are currently studying are operating on a timescale of decades, maybe even a century or two, at best—not the millennia within which geoscientists typically frame Earth's catastrophes.

We must keep the changes we are now observing in perspective. Consider that the last time large amounts of carbon were dumped into the atmosphere, about 55 million years ago in an event called the Paleocene-Eocene Thermal Maximum, it occurred over a period of several thousand years. If this last extinction occurred over a period of five thousand years and the catastrophic extinctions and environmental change we now face occurs in one hundred or two hundred years, then one can sense the devastating nature and speed of what is underway.

While humankind, if we act boldly, may have the ability to culturally adapt to what is underway, many species on the planet will not have that opportunity.

The current environmental changes are not merely tragic, but catastrophic, something on an entirely different order of magnitude than previous disasters in which humankind has played a hand. Humankind is poised through our actions to create the first planetary catastrophe of human genesis in the history of our cosmos.

The real question is can we act boldly to stop this global catastrophe? Honestly, I do not know. Maybe—it depends, for there is much that we cannot control or predict as this catastrophe unfolds. What we must address is the necessity for immediate changes in our everyday mundane life activities: reduce use of gasoline-fueled vehicles and dependence on coal-generated electricity, recalibrate our comfort indices and our overall habits of consumption, and move from fulfilling advertisement-induced wants to fulfilling needs.

THE DIFFICULTY OF DEALING WITH IMMEDIATE CHANGES

If we can make these not-easy changes in our everyday lives, for they are indeed difficult in the kind of cornucopia cultures we find ourselves immersed in today, we can act responsibly and respectfully to the life that surrounds us on our Mother Earth. In order to accomplish these easily acknowledged but difficult to actualize activities, serious examination of the wisdom that resides in the cultures and worldviews of the indigenous peoples of the planet must take place. Again, this suggestion does not mean we should go back to the past, or, as some might say, live in the past. Such linear thinking about our human history is, indeed, a large part of the problem.

The fundamental question we must ask is can we act boldly, irrespective of a guaranteed outcome? The answer is yes. We have little choice if we want to leave good things for future generations. We must examine the wisdom that remains—even today—in the cultures and worldviews of the indigenous peoples of the planet. If we look carefully, we can find new paths for cultures of life enhancement among the old ways. Humankind may indeed still claim an inheritance thought destroyed and discarded by those possessing what Kirkpatrick Sale calls the "culture of conquest." What we desperately need are the knowledges of peoples who developed lifeways over many generations in places they called home. People are likely to take this assessment as hyperbole, and that would be a mistake. To construe this statement as exaggeration would require ignorance, selfishness, or disingenuousness.

Fortunately, I see more ignorance than either selfishness or disingenuousness in the world, and that is good news. For those suffering from ignorance can be informed and their questions can be answered straightforwardly. Those acting selfishly or dedicated to misleading half-truths are likely to either claim ignorance in their rationalizations for participation in an impoverishing and deadly culture or lay claim to a pseudo-Darwinian naturalism that is merely a shallow ex post facto historical truism, a sort of Panglossian "best of all possible worlds" assessment of the present.

If some find what follows simplistic, such an assessment can only be made from an ideal—in other words, abstract—rationalist standpoint. For there is much that humankind seems capable of intelligently grasping when we put our mind to it, but it is quite another thing to equate knowledge with doing the right thing. If we can judge by human behavior, especially that of modern humankind, the notion advanced by some that we can easily equate knowing with doing seems suspect.

The indigenous ingenuity—or, as Haskell Indian Nations University graduate Curtis Kekahbah of the Kaw Nation called it, the indigenuity: the ability to solve pressing life issues facing humankind now by situating our solutions in Earth-based local indigenous deep spatial knowledges—of tribal peoples constitutes a practical merger of knowing with doing. Their lifeways embody knowing as doing—a wonderful doing, not at all simplistic or easy, but an ability to work with what they have available and the wisdom to ensure, such as they can, that they can continue doing it.

Tribal peoples have a keen ability to handle abstraction: the cosmologies, metaphysics, and physics of any number of American Indian and Alaska Native peoples show levels of sophisticated abstraction. However, even in our complex exercises of logic and metaphysics, the relations, processes, and experiences we recognize in our attempts to gain understanding take precedence over pure abstraction. While we live in a society today rich in ideas, images, and ideologies, what we lack and desperately need is practical knowledge about living well brought about by a lifetime of attentiveness to something other than our own human-produced culture.

If we look at recent human behavior, say for the last five hundred years—some would go back as far as two thousand or even five thousand years—it seems at first glance reasonable to conclude that we, human beings, are a weed species. The invasive character of a global capitalist consumer economic system and culture give many of humankind the appearance of weeds. Everywhere we go—everywhere we develop—the populations of other Native and often ancient species decline. However, we need to be careful about the use of the word *we*, for the good news is that collectively we—all of humankind—have not behaved like weeds. Until very recently, in many cases, cultures have existed in environments and ecosystems on the planet for thousands of years in quite sustainable symbiotic relationships with places. Our problem is not biological in "nature," but cultural in character.

Not everyone on the planet has lived in invasive weed–like cultures—a precious few still do not—and many peoples remember or recollect what life in a world without weeds was like. Saving the Earth with indigenous knowledges will require a serious examination and reconstruction of the experiential knowledge of Native peoples: it will require getting people out of the physical and metaphysical boxes in which they live and think. In order to live in life-enhancing relations, humankind in industrial and postindustrial societies must move beyond their self-imposed physical, emotional, intellectual, and spiritual imprisonment.

In spite of the increasing homogeneity of our media-interrelated world, there are still substantial lands and waters of the Earth that are, in a profound sociohistorical sense, off the map for most of humanity. In these places, off the map with peoples off the clock, so to speak, we can observe destruction and hope.

DESTRUCTION AND HOPE

Adrian Cowell's poignant 1990 documentary film, *The Decade of Destruction*, about the ecological and cultural devastation brought to the rainforest landscapes of interior Brazil in the mid-1980s illustrates this point. When a young boy of a homesteading settler family is feared kidnapped by Indians, the father and others searching for the boy contact a poacher deep in the forests for information regarding the stolen child. The poacher is sought out because of his knowledge of the little-known and rarely seen tribe the Eru-Eu-Wau-Wau, who are suspected of taking the boy. Since the only places where the poacher can find the endangered and obviously poorly protected cats that he kills is in the homeland of the Indians, he has firsthand knowledge of the Indians. The only places where the wild cats and the wildlife, otherwise threatened by development, are found is on the same lands where one finds indigenous peoples.

The reasonable and hopeful conclusion is that humankind is not, so to speak, hardwired biologically to behave like weeds, demonstrating invasive behavior at the expense of other life and biological diversity. It should be counted as good news, a reason for hope, that across the planet where we find the long demonized and maligned "wild savages," people basically tribal in character, we can still find wildlife. The bad news is that our fascination with technology in isolation from any attentiveness to the life around us is now clearly threatening life that until recently we could not imagine losing, or should we say more accurately, destroying.

Humans ought to take seriously the lifeways of tribal peoples throughout the planet precisely because more often than not they have lived quite well with other life, with biological diversity, much better than modern industrial or postindustrial societies. The myopic Western view of progress has brought not only ourselves, but all of our relatives and their homes—the land, air, and water—impoverished and diminished biological diversity.

Before scientists and scholars get too exacerbated by these claims, keep in mind such claims do not require or even mean to suggest that we did not make mistakes (for example, Cahokia and Chaco Canyon) or sometimes needed reminding that we were not in control of the natural world (for example, Anasazi culture). Earlier societies, not only civilizations, made mistakes, but it appears that some learned from their errors. The evidence that modern, and now postmodern, societies have been built on an unsustainable, indeed, a destructive foundation, is daily becoming hard to ignore.

This dark assessment comes not from the pages of the so often disparaged "tree-hugger" or "whole-wheat freak" organizations; it comes from scientists, "objective" scientists, folks who quantify and measure everything. Wisdom-keepers within our tribal traditions have passed down warnings and prophesies about the world in which we live that correspond quite well with what scientists are now finding out about the current state of planet Earth.

The fact that these forecasts converge is only surprising to those who fail to appreciate the current state of environmental science and the living legacy of spiritual knowledges maintained in tribal traditions about the condition of our Mother Earth.

Scientists, who in many cases seem to epitomize Western worldviews, are beginning to sound alerts as a result of their work and research. Many scientists are alarmed, as they should be. They, too, are sending warnings about catastrophic changes that seem to be on their way to the Earth's biosphere and geography. It is time to make a strategic alliance, but one led by peoples who think of the planet and our places here in the big picture—indigenous thinkers who know places and the powers that reside there. In order to live well, humankind will have to reexamine how we find our cultures once again in the land and waters, places experienced as homes, as opposed to Internet cafés and shopping malls.

YOU MIGHT BE MINERS, BUT WE ARE NOT CANARIES

Indigenous peoples are now paying an extraordinarily high price in their cultures, landscapes, and seascapes for the myopic arrogance of industrial and postindustrial cultures built on the modern myth of humankind's mastery over nature. Honestly, I am not sure what this human-made global catastrophe says about justice—environmental or any other kind, for that matter. I do know that I do not want to hear another miner's canary metaphor. It is incredibly self-serving for those from afar geographically and culturally to liken indigenous peoples fighting to maintain their unique lifeways and identities to alarms for societies that have demonstrated little respect for nature and Natives. We are not canaries in your service, but peoples carrying messages from relatives in what John Mohawk correctly described as the complex web of life.

It is difficult to fathom a worldview that considers humankind in charge of all of creation when human history and experience clearly suggest we either cannot or have no desire to control ourselves. One indigenous approach to mitigating the environmental chaos that a civilized fixation with control has brought to life on Earth would be to think in terms of cooperation and coordination with the balance of nature beyond our human selves. Some of humankind have created a situation that seems almost impossible to address, but this perceived impossibility is primarily the result of three factors: ignorance, inattentiveness, and a lack of imagination.

Of these three factors, the most difficult to address will be the lack of imagination, or, as I stressed earlier, the fostering of indigenuity. With the help of our allies—private foundations, nongovernmental organizations, some attentive federal agencies and offices, and good folks disillusioned with a culture to which they no longer want to belong—tribal colleges will play a crucial role in creating future generations of indigenous thinkers capable of exercising indigenuity. Indigenous thinkers, as our histories confirm, recognize the present as both the distillation of the past and the catalyst for the future. The world is not a simple environment, and the problems we face cannot be addressed by reductionist logic, scientific or otherwise.

The global-burning issue we currently face might be better addressed through adopting complexity models of the current situation. By doing so, we might move away from thinking about a single solution for the problem we face and toward thinking about our participation in an emerging world where we do not wring our hands and fail to act, but act even in little ways, in personal choices, to contribute to emerging systems—in other words, societal properties—that might slow the accelerating decline in the diversity of life we are now witnessing. We have nothing to lose but the hubris that promotes the thought that somehow we, humankind, are in control. What is gained is an entrée to indigenous knowledges—implicitly complex systems of knowledge—that will never claim to know it all, but will claim to know something: something about our relations, the necessity for respect, and, most importantly, the inalienability of responsibilities humankind must accept if we and our relatives are to live well on Mother Earth.

CHAPTER FOUR

A Red Alert for Indigenous Action in Life-Enhancing Cultures

No single work or author could cover the depth and breadth of indigenous knowledges and their sources on Earth. The diversity of life constituting Mother Earth's life system precludes simplistic one-size-fits-all technological solutions to the climate problems human activity has produced. We now have the opportunity to promote the development of indigenuity. These deep spatial knowledges exist globally. By this I mean that these indigenous knowledges are found everywhere on the planet where peoples and places have maintained long-standing symbiotic relations. These local knowledges are emergent in a nature-culture nexus, a sort of first-order global positioning system, or, in other words, an experiential positioning system (EPS). People in possession of these EPSs and knowledges, like the fishing peoples of the Northwest Coast, the Navajo (Diné) and Pueblo farmers of the Southwest, and medicine people throughout North America, know where they are without the aid of a satellite-driven coordinate system.

Indigenous knowledges are situated in and emergent from life systems—environments and ecosystems—where peoples continue to find their lifeways. These local knowledges, which are situated in a continuum of change and experience, serve as a provocation to challenge and unsettle those forward-looking, progress-infatuated, linear thinkers who are unappreciative of the possibility that useful knowledge resides in tribal lifeways. If realism in a general sense denotes something about our daily lives—how we live—then there can be no more crucial climate-change discussion than one regarding our daily lives.

WHERE WE START: THE SACRED IN THE WORLD

At the first annual Impact of Changing Environments on Indigenous Peoples symposium held at Haskell Indian Nations University, Angayuqaq Oscar Kawagley opened his incredible report about the dire situation facing his Alaska Native relatives with a plea to the Spiritual Person of the universe. For some, beginning a report on climate-change impacts with such a statement might seem odd or out of place given the very pressing practical issues facing the indigenous peoples of Alaska and the entire circumpolar arctic region, but for indigenous thinkers, such an invocation is expected—indeed required. For most indigenous thinkers, the practical questions regarding our human lives and the other life on this planet could hardly be expected to be addressed effectively without such awareness and acknowledgment.

In Euchee (Yuchi) traditions, and all of the indigenous North American traditions with which I have had the good fortune to come into contact, the recognition of practical knowledges and their goals is based on an acknowledgment and respect—an attentiveness—to the sacred in the world surrounding us. Our American Indian and

Alaska Native customs and ceremonial practices convey the character of the sacred powers surrounding us. For the most part, we have no tradition of theological writings and treatises. While this has frustrated many from outside our cultural traditions who have sought to understand us, the hesitancy to record the most crucial and the most practical of our knowledges suggests something about the applicability of these knowledges.

If, as Vine Deloria Jr. formulated the issue, sacred knowledge is most fundamentally about the life of *people* in relationship to a *place*, especially sacred lands, and their resulting *personality*, then such knowledge in its practical particulars is known best to the *peoples* of that *place*. The unfortunate situation for societies that begin to behave as if knowledge primarily resides in words (images) in a book is that they forget we had words before books, stories before books, and analytic abilities before we had texts. For humankind, words—languages—were never only about us, but signifiers of our rich relationships in a complex and diverse world.

Because we do not all live in the same place on this beautiful blue-green planet, our relationships, languages, and, for the sake of simplicity, let us say religions, vary with the landscapes and seascapes in which we dwell. Ecological pluralism, with some notable exceptions, explains our religious diversity, and because our "religions" are situated in the world, in the universe, not as idealists or materialists understand their religion or lack thereof in the Western tradition, we have saved ourselves from religious wars.

As Red Jacket, Tecumseh, Sitting Bull, Chief Joseph, and today elders such as Albert White Hat and Kawagley point out, indigenous "religious" traditions were and remain largely bound up in experiential examinations and demonstrations of the complex web of relationships that surround us and that many indigenous languages refer to with multiple meanings—sometimes all at once. Our attentiveness to this living world, including what Kawagley called "the Spiritual Person of the universe," is promoted through custom, habit, ceremony, and language, not words or arguments from a book. Then and now, the best source for understanding creation and the Creator is embodied in the experiential features of our actions: the deepest insights are gained in our doing.

The acknowledgment and respect for the living spiritual foundation of the world speaks most directly to what some rigorous scientists in Western institutions find most problematic in indigenous traditions and knowledges: prayer. There is much that could be said about the sense of the sacred that permeates North American indigenous traditions and worldviews, but words are ultimately inadequate to convey what is known through experience. This opinion does not denigrate the power of words. I have lived and worked with few people who take words as seriously as do American Indians and Alaska Natives. Rather, it tells us about the experiential power of the sacred.

The dualisms or dichotomies between the spiritual and material, culture and nature, subjective and objective, sacred and profane that operate so deeply in the Western worldview appear largely absent from the American Indian and Alaska Native worldviews of which I am familiar. Indigenous traditions recognize the sacred in a world simultaneously spiritual and physical. Those who find this view problematic should remember it is *their* problem, not *ours*. Humankind possesses a wide variety of opinions about what many call "religious" questions, and fortunately, in many of our tribal traditions, such debates and disputations are not *our* concern.

The Seneca leader Red Jacket's famous declaration, "We never quarrel about religion," when facing the preaching of those intent on converting him and other Indians to Christianity, captures something we ought to all think about today. Chief Joseph responded in a similar fashion when asked by a member of an official US commission visiting the Wallowa Valley in Oregon why churches were not allowed on Nez Perce lands: "They [churches] will teach us to quarrel about God, as Catholics and Protestants do on the Nez Perce Reservation and other places. We do not want to do that. We may quarrel sometimes about things on Earth, but we never quarrel about the Great Spirit. We do not want to learn that."

As "uncivilized" as we Natives allegedly were, we can take great pride in the fact that we have no history of intertribal religious wars in our collective past. There is little evidence that American Indians and Alaska Natives ever waged or justified war based on the fact that another nation or people had a different idea of the sacred and the way of honoring and interacting with the power and powers that animate and move through this world.

Our tribal traditions have no place for religious proselytizing: it is perceived as rude to tell someone how they ought to pray and to whom. Yet, irrespective of one's religion, spiritual tradition, or lack of either, we are, as many of my northern plains friends say, *mitakua oysin*, "all related," in this world. For this reason alone, humankind ought to think deeply about the relationships and processes some of us have so greatly disturbed. A good deal of the biology of this planet, as we have known it, is now threatened because of the global extension of carbon-based industries and the lifestyles it promotes. It is not accidental that many of the environmental threats, especially those related to climate change, have coincided with a global expansion of carbon-based industrialization that until recently was thought to have the capacity to solve most of humankind's problems.

Indigenous peoples adapted, we innovated, but now many of us face climate threats so severe that our cultural identities are threatened. Humankind has entered the twenty-first century with much more to think about than the global economic crisis moving through the richest Western nations of the world. As climatic, environmental, educational, and political problems emerge daily across the globe that turn out to be global in character, it is time to have some difficult discussions. The peoples on the planet who had the least to do with the climate crisis and yet are the most vulnerable to its destructive impacts should rightly lead these discussions.

THE NECESSITY OF DIFFICULT DISCUSSIONS

Chief Joseph acknowledged, "We may quarrel about things on Earth"; however, this Red Alert is an invitation to start a dialogue without being quarrelsome. We American Indians and Alaska Natives have been on the receiving end of Western ideas, opinions, and colonial institutions for five hundred years. Now we face a situation on the planet where Native voices must be heard in order to avert or hopefully minimize the deadly events emerging.

Native peoples are capable of stating more clearly and directly, minus romantic or melodramatic embellishment, what civilizations seem to have lost in their marches of progress—insights regarding the ways in which humans might live in a more life-enhancing manner with recognition and appreciation of the diversity of life that surrounds us on this planet. In a world where a good number of us think being connected means having our cell phones, BlackBerries, and iPhones charged, it is likely that we forget about and become disconnected from our immediate environment beyond the technology at our fingertips.

Honesty requires an admission: many of us quite simply have not been paying attention. Some of humankind apparently had to make the Earth a place where the planetary life crisis we now face could be tangibly felt before many of us could recognize this fundamental environmental crisis. In this admission lies hope: this global climate change has less to do with our human nature and much more to do with human cultures. The incredibly high cost of this climate change to our Mother Earth must be understood as related to humankind's development of societies and cultures disconnected in fundamental ways from the landscapes and seascapes, the places where they are situated.

In the United States, indigenous peoples, American Indians, and Alaska Natives continue to maintain cultural features emergent from the landscapes and seascapes they call home. Indigenous cultures in the broadest sense—

material, nonmaterial, and behavioral—were, and many amazingly remain, emergent from their environments. Again, it is ironic that the peoples on the planet who participated least in the making of this global environmental crisis—the indigenous peoples of the circumpolar arctic region, the desert Southwest of the United States, the Great Lakes region of North America, and, indeed, tribal peoples throughout the world—will immediately and most directly suffer the impacts of the looming climate crises. At the same time, these unique peoples and places offer humankind some of the best insights about how to address the Mother Earth's present situation. Tribal lifeways can remind us of the imperative to reconstitute a life-enhancing nature-culture nexus in the places where we live.

Life, in the broadest sense, on Earth can ill afford the lifeways and worldview increasingly marketed around the world. Given the catastrophe humankind and all of our ecological relatives now face, after centuries of human efforts to make the natural world fit us, it is realistic, not romantic in a Rousseauian sense, to look circumspectly at cultures that fit the unique environments of their homelands. Fortunately, it appears growing numbers of non-indigenous persons are recognizing that they have a moral and even a self-interest-based responsibility to listen to what indigenous peoples have to say about the current condition of our Mother Earth and to involve us in decision-making processes beyond the minimum treaty-based requirements that will affect our lives.

In one of the most exciting developments, indigenous peoples are beginning to talk to each other and make treaties between our own nations. Although few members of the dominant society of the United States paid any attention, we now have a United League of Indigenous Nations. Meeting in the homeland of the Lummi Nation on August 1, 2007, eleven indigenous nations reached agreement on the Treaty of Indigenous Nations, and in Denver, Colorado, on November 15, 2007, ratified and signed this historic treaty. Since the United States no longer has any interest in signing treaties with indigenous nations, and especially, as the Kyoto Protocol treaty demonstrated, those treaties dealing with climate change and carbon dioxide emissions, it appears the First Nations of this land called America may well have the opportunity to negotiate treaties among themselves and with other indigenous peoples around the world.

Indigenous peoples should establish their own carbon dioxide and pollution-reduction protocols. We need to compare notes and share stories with our relatives from the Four Directions around the globe. Although token acknowledgment is given to the Haudenosaunee for their influence on the so-called Founding Fathers' ideas regarding American democracy, it is now time for the First Nations of North America to actively demonstrate their ancient democratic traditions. Indigenous nations must exercise a sovereignty that throughout many traditions conceptualizes and expresses democracy as life-enhancing ecological practices.

Today humankind must address the dominant life-threatening features of cultural traditions that identified "civilization" with the ideas of a human-controlled natural world, the central importance of humankind's material comfort and convenience, and modern economic systems—

capitalist and socialist alike—that construe the natural world as consisting of resources as opposed to relatives. As Oren Lyons, Onondaga faith-keeper, remarked at a ceremony held on the Ellipse across from the White House on the twenty-fifth anniversary of Earth Day, it makes a crucial difference whether humankind thinks of the natural world as consisting of resources or relatives.

If one wants to explore a fundamental paradigm shift, consider how human behavior in the most technologically advanced societies on the planet would have to change if one treated the balance of nature beyond our human selves as relatives, not resources. Humankind has for too long treated the natural world beyond ourselves like automated teller machines (ATMs), and the withdrawals far exceed the deposits. Try treating your human relatives like ATMs and see if you are not put in your place very quickly. You will be reminded, sometimes very harshly, that you are part of a family, a social network that requires respectful interaction if one hopes to reap the many benefits of membership.

The material natural resources we impersonally manage, or, typically, let someone else take care of, can be so easily taken for granted that we have become inattentive and unaware of these natural relatives and relationships that constitute the world in which our human-engineered and increasingly artificial and unsustainable environments are built. The global integration of social institutions committed to environmentally life-threatening economic activities, as opposed to life-enhancing activities, has resulted in a growing number of humankind participating in global burning.

WARNING SIGNS

Our climate is clearly changing as a result of the behavior of a good number of humankind on the planet. However, it appears that the human behavior responsible for what can reasonably be called a catastrophe in progress is not changing. Startling newspaper headlines are becoming commonplace: "Global Carbon Levels Spiraling," reported the Tuesday, May 22, 2007, edition of *USA Today*.[1] The same paper the next day featured a front-page article discussing how exchange-traded mutual funds are investing in water—clean, drinkable water—for it will undoubtedly be a scarce resource in the future.[2] The indicators of deadly and near-catastrophic environmental changes across every geographic region of the world are so numerous, it is difficult and numbing, if not depressing, to enumerate what indigenous wisdom-keepers and life scientists are now observing.

The growing list of casualties to plants, animals, fragile ecosystems, and human communities is staggering. The most recent Red List of threatened species released by the International Union for Conversation of Nature (IUCN) in May of 2006 confirms that the rate of extinction is indeed speeding up. In order to put the raw numbers of threatened species in perspective, an IUCN news release noted, "This includes one in three amphibians and a quarter of the world's coniferous trees, on top of the one in eight birds and one in four mammals known to be in jeopardy."[3] In short, land, air, water, and life, which depends on the first three elements, are under siege by humans guided by a worldview with roots so deeply embedded in the ideas of Western civilization that it is part of an unconscious, taken-for-granted "reality" that has become second nature—or, more accurately, second to nature.

None of this should be shocking to citizens of the United States since their institutions—economic, political, religious, educational, and now media, with its unprecedented growth in satellite-, digital-, and Internet-driven information technology—promote life-destroying consumer behavior fostered by a myopic view of civilization. Certainly, the West has no historical monopoly on the idea or experience of civilization. Nevertheless, the West does have an unparalleled five-centuries-long involvement in a global colonization project that still reverberates and echoes today, especially in a Western-influenced dream of a globally integrated political economy (China now included)—an integration manufactured in such a way that no place or peoples on this planet are left unscathed. The move to unify the world based on universal truths and inalienable rights, which are continually reduced to economic market laws and forces by neoconservatives and neoliberals alike, is so uncritically empire-centric that it makes George Lucas's *Star Wars* look like a naive view of future planetary domination.

George Orwell and Aldous Huxley, as it turned out, were each half right. *Big Brother* is no longer a fictional literary character, but the consummate unreal reality television show. And while the pharmaceutical companies have yet to perfect the universal anxiety and unhappiness cure-all soma, they do offer a wide variety of drugs to address our modern anxieties and stress-related illnesses. For his part, Orwell, no doubt, would marvel at a popular political culture that has made overt surveillance a secondary consideration in modern societies where people increasingly get their information and knowledge of world events through centralized and homogenized media conglomerates. If you can ensure that everyone, to a large extent, sees the world the same way because they are looking not at the world, but at the commercial media's uniform representation of the world, then ensuring control is made much easier.

Huxley's image of the brave new world has held up fairly well too, especially in the United States. For example, couples now shop for genetically designed children, preferably alphas, while American adults ingest antidepressant drugs at an all-time high and young people seek the latest sensory stimulation and thrills at the "feelies," now denominated *raves*. The most amazing thing about Huxley's classic work is how much of it is part of the everyday life of many in modern societies today, or, as some young cybercitizens might say, the B-Rave new world. The social psychological state of the people of the United States, especially the young who seek a sort of temporary and drug-induced communal feeling in anonymous crowds, provides one more compelling reason why Americans would do well to examine indigenous ideas of community found among the First Peoples of North America.

REPLACING MODERN MYTHOLOGY WITH INDIGENOUS REALISM

Advanced "civilized" societies, with their powerful technologies and rationality, evidence an adherence to a body of myths and romanticism that eclipses anything imagined in tribal worldviews and lifeways. The increasing impoverishment of life on Earth alone suggests the irony in modern society's inevitable casting of American Indian lifeways and worldviews as full of myth and romance. Primary among the myths to which modern humankind faithfully adheres is the notion of their moral and intellectual superiority among all other living beings on the planet—a self-evident superiority in part engendered by our apparent control and manipulation of the natural world.

However, if romanticism denotes impracticality and unrealistic aspirations, can there be a more romantic myth than the idea that civilized humankind can always rise above nature through the exercise of reason and the application of technology? When one listens to debates about the two-centuries-old ideas of capitalism and socialism and their respective merits in producing wealth, it seems strangely surreal, for the wealth both economic theories speak of values so little the natural world and our natural human relationship to it. Humankind now needs a good dose of indigenous realism that demonstrates the miseducative character of the dualisms, dichotomies, and categorizations that dominate the thinking and activities of growing numbers of humans on the planet today.

Progress is a powerful idea when associated with societies and history, for it is imbued with positive connotations such as happiness, comfort, convenience, wealth, freedom, and the denotation of technological advance and economic development. No one wants to be told they are against progress. A substantial part of its power and attractiveness results from the fact that it is overwhelmingly anthropocentric—literally human-centered—in character.

Progress is something humans make and do. At the most fundamental level, it denotes improvement, something we do not expect plants, other animals, or other features of nature to do. The idea of progress plays into a realism regarding nature that modern humankind is only now beginning to fully appreciate. It encourages the use of something—reality—before we really know "it," or at least the central feature progressive thinkers place in their natural world: ourselves.

Indigenous knowledges begin with a realization that today seems counterintuitive: we can only know ourselves through our relationships with relatives in the natural world—the nature-culture nexus. Such knowledges are the result of both introspection and extrospection. It is not an either/or proposition. Indigenous realism suggests a dynamic and active construction of knowledge.

At the Planning for Seven Generations Conference in the spring of 2008, cosponsored by the National Center for Atmospheric Research, the University Corporation for Atmospheric Research, and the American Indian and Alaska Native Climate Change Working Group, Craig Fleener, a Vuntut Gwitchin from Fort Yukon, Alaska, illustrated the character of indigenous knowledges marvelously. Fleener stated:

> We don't just talk about climate change because we heard about it on TV or read about it in a magazine or somebody mentioned it in school and everybody is scared of this thing that is coming. We experience it every day of our lives.
>
> If you live in a city and you are rushing from building to building, you probably don't even notice that it is happening. You run from home to jump in

your car, drive twenty miles, and go to work. You get off work, go to the store, and do whatever you do. You go back home. You don't even notice the changes. But when you spend all of the time that you have outside—you know seventy-four degrees below zero doesn't stop us from going outside…So we have these experiences and we notice when things happen.

One of the reasons why you can truly consider the indigenous lifeways as a true science is because our life is a science. Everything that we do is an experiment. Every single time we do what we are told to do by our elders,…we either take that information, we go with it, or we try to change it a little bit. We add to it. We manipulate what has been given down to us. So it is truly a scientific measure, a little bit to see if we improve this thing.[4]

Fleener expressed what I call indigenous realism, a living system of knowledge, one that is not frozen in time, but a deep experiential knowledge that is capable of change and innovation, the ability to figure out what works in a particular place for the people of that place. One advantage of knowledges arrived at in the processes of experiments in living, as Fleener described them, is that such knowledges result in worldviews that are intrinsically open-ended or unbounded, much like the complex environments and diverse life from which these indigenous scientific knowledges emerge.

Humankind must look around and see what the places of our planet can teach us. Our vision is obscured by the walls of the boxes within which we increasingly live and, not surprisingly, think. This Red Alert reminds those living and thinking in boxes that we still have peoples residing in a nature-culture nexus, peoples who are still deeply connected to places and who possess practical, life-enhancing knowledges desperately needed today.

CHAPTER FIVE

Indigenous Knowledges:
Where We Touch the Earth

Some will find the proposal to save the planet with indigenous knowledges incredible: What an unrealistic reverie! What a modern-American-sounding hubris-ridden declaration. Most of those individuals will never turn a page in this book. But for those willing to consider that useful knowledge and wisdom for humankind might be found in indigenous tribal traditions, honesty requires that such a claim be explained.

INDIGENOUS KNOWLEDGES:
COLLABORATIVE SYSTEMS OF KNOWING

The proposal to use indigenous knowledges to save the Earth denotes knowledge as something not passively found in "nature," but something found in the experiential exploration of our human place within the natural world. The Native insight that indigenous knowledges should not be strictly understood as human constructions, but rather as collaborations, is worth emphasizing. Indigenous knowledges in this sense are emergent from the nature-culture nexus. Consequently, indigenous knowledges are a set of relations and relationships situated in our life experiences, which vary as we move through what physicists would call space-time.

The increasing impoverishment of life on Earth is overwhelmingly a cultural product. After a five-centuries-old imposition of Eurocentric institutions around the globe, the world might benefit from a serious examination and discussion of indigenous ideas found among the First Peoples of North America. It is ironic that American Indian lifeways and worldviews, exceptional for their practicality, are inevitably cast by modern societies as full of myth and romanticized recollections. Indigenous ingenuity (indigenuity) can help us deal with the fundamental cultural crisis that threatens much of Mother Earth's life system, for the global burning we are immersed in is ultimately about how a great number of humankind currently lives—it is about the lifestyles that have been sold to us.

New Age secrets and formulae, and exoticized platitudes of mythological tribal origin, are absent in these pages. What is offered here is neither exotic nor romantic, but practical and philosophical. What the world needs today is a good dose of indigenous realism. We need knowledges that emerged through hundreds and often thousands of years of interaction with ecosystems and larger environments. Humankind can benefit from indigenous knowledges, identified as realistic, precisely because they often resulted in sustainable life-enhancing social institutions and material cultures.

Indigenous knowledges are grounded in the human realization that the life that surrounds us can teach us valuable lifeway lessons, if we pay attention to our relationships and interactions with the land, air, water, and other-than-human living beings. The hard-fact skeptics will likely ridicule any such claim, but their attitude is largely explained by ignorance. For these empiricists have typically lived the vast majority of their lives inside human-designed and -constructed interiors. Human beings who spend time with animals or live a large part of their lives outside the walls of man-made buildings and exercise attentiveness to their environment universally affirm the existence of intraspecies communication systems.

Current scientific research on animal communication overwhelmingly verifies the existence of complex communication systems. Honesty and humility require us to acknowledge that indigenous knowledge, in its diverse substance and structure, is the result of collaboration, a respectful partnership, between us and our many other-than-human relatives. Several tribal elders I have known have been almost matter-of-fact about their ability to exercise interspecies communication with animals.

During an advisory board meeting for the Haskell Environmental Research Studies Center at Haskell Indian Nations University in 1996, the subject of the wolf population in the northern Rocky Mountains came up. I can still remember, at the close of the meeting, respected North Cheyenne elder the late Bill Tallbull telling some of us that when he went home, it was time for him to have a face-to-face visit with the wolves he shared the land with. As I recall, he said, "I'll sit out in 'my backyard' and wait for them to come, then we will visit."

I have often wondered what people thought Tallbull was saying. I have no doubt that he was going to have a visit—they were going to communicate. I cannot say how they were going to communicate, and he did not volunteer the information. But having been lucky enough to know Tallbull, I took him at his word.

Vine Deloria Jr. told me Tallbull would often relate information like this after a meeting. Maybe he did not want to call attention to himself by announcing his intentions openly to very many people, and/or maybe he knew some might not understand nor respect how he communicated with his other-than-human relatives. Either way, his remarks and soft-spoken, matter-of-fact way of relating this information were representative of the humility embodied by indigenous wisdom-keepers, a humility required by the recognition that within indigenous knowledge systems, the knowledge we humans possess, incomplete as it must always be, is the product of our relatedness to the complex web of life. Indigenous knowledges are not a human construction, but, more importantly, a gift given to us, when we pay attention, by the relatives who surround us.

Indigenous knowledges, as the ancient traditions of many peoples around the planet remind us, reside in the land, in the life that constitutes the ecologies in which we participate, and dwells within the Earth's environments. Modern humankind too conveniently and mindlessly thinks of these ecosystems and environments as "nature," but nature as a grand abstraction, the idea and unreality to which modern humankind claims to desire to be so close. Yet, all the while, institutions and activities, especially those found in industrial and postindustrial cultures, seek to insulate the very same nature-seekers from the immediate and particular reality of the nature found in our own backyards—the lived-in world experienced deeply by our human ancestors, albeit not by choice, but by necessity.

The result of our ancestors' deep experience, their existential situation, was hardly romantic in a Rousseauian noble-savage sense, but it was beautiful. Around the planet, many tribal peoples possess a sense of place in landscapes and seascapes that remains palpable and very real in a spiritual and physical way. They dwell in a sense of place, beauty, and belonging that remains centered in the same world that besets humankind in modern societies with frustration and trouble. Modern humankind experiences both precisely because beauty, belonging, and sense of place have become control-demanding and technology-dependent products that preoccupy the attention and activities of many today to such an extent that these things preclude the recognition of the real beauty that surrounds us.

The advantage our ancestors possessed was that they did not operate with the delusion that they ought to be in control of the natural world beyond their human selves. In place of measuring the good life in terms of products, many indigenous traditions recognize and express the good life as a process—active and complementary participation in natural processes not of our design. Consequently, their focus was on finding ways to live in environments, or, let us say, within environments, instead of expending the energies modern humans devote to changing environments.

Indigenous knowledges offer insights into living well on Mother Earth because they are fundamentally cooperative and collaborative constructions. These knowledges are in the strictest sense of the term ecological in character, as Greg Cajete pointed out in his beautiful book *Look to the Mountain*. There is hope for this living planet, if we can find ways to live in a manner that encourages us to pay attention to the world we live in, or, as Deloria was inclined to say, "the world we used to live in." Hopefulness resides in the fact that the world, in spite of our attempts to control and engineer it, is still alive outside the conceptual categories we impose on it and beyond the boxes we exist in and communicate through.

THE WAY WE LIVE IS THE PROBLEM

The primary problem we face today is the way a great number of humankind live. If we examine the evidence across nearly every dimension of our natural environment— the land, air, water, biology, and their interactions in the Earth's biosphere—it is impossible to come to any other conclusion.

Unfortunately, once this realization soaks in to our consciousness, the magnitude of the problem can be overwhelming, for it is indeed multidimensional, as it affects nearly every aspect of our lives. It now appears that merely slowing down or reducing what we have been doing—in terms of cutting back on our consumption of fossil fuels, for example—simply forestalls an inevitable and rapidly approaching confrontation with the fact that humankind needs to find better ways to live.

The catastrophe humankind is making requires fundamental reappraisals of the means and ends to which human life is directed. This will no doubt sound grandiose to many people, but I challenge skeptics to examine the climate-change issues. Examine the global burning in which we engage, and one will find a rather amazing unanimity among indigenous knowledge-bearers across the planet and scientists across many disciplines about the magnitude of this crisis. After a centuries-long colonial imposition of Eurocentric notions of civilization and progress on indigenous peoples and their landscapes and seascapes throughout the world, the export of a fundamentally Western, universal worldview and way of life has resulted in some of humankind drastically changing the face of this planet in ways that will be catastrophic.

Continuing global "development" with the same worldview and institutions that have produced the deadly global situation we now face reminds me of one of the popular definitions of insanity: the act of trying the same thing over and over again while expecting to get a different result each time. Considering the climate-change trajectory on which the planet currently finds itself, the proposal to critically examine the knowledge and wisdom of the indigenous peoples of North America for insights on how humans might live well and enhance life on the planet seems prudent.

Saving the planet with indigenous knowledges will require the development of indigenuity—the ability to draw on insights found deep in tribal cultures—not only in North America, but around the world, and apply them in innovative ways to practical problems we face in our everyday lives. This will be crucial during the next several decades. Once we rid ourselves of the incredibly powerful but abstract notions of a linear temporal universal history and its attendant conceptions of progress and civilization, the proposal to save the Earth with indigenous knowledges will be seen as a very sane suggestion. Hopefully, modern humankind has reached a place and time where we can recognize that we must look beyond our notions of civilization and its presumed cultural superiority and look outside our cultures for solutions to problems that our cultures, in the broadest sense, and idea of civilization have created.

Lessons regarding how we might live in a sustainable nature-culture nexus surround us. In North America, the legacy of Hohokam, the current life system of the Menominee forests, and now the exploration of wind energy on the northern plains illustrate the power of thinking indigenously.

INDIGENUITY—PAST, PRESENT, AND FUTURE

Past: Hohokam—A Story of Water and Power

Few people know that Phoenix, Arizona, and the surrounding suburbs sit on top of one of the most extensive and sophisticated irrigation systems in the world. Not the modern system that has developed over the course of the last century, but the system that reached its zenith two centuries before Cristóbal Colón (Columbus), lost somewhere in the Bahamas, was discovered by the Taino Indians. This system constituted the physical foundation of what is called the Hohokam cultural complex, or, with considerable justification, might be called Hohokam civilization.

Hohokam bears nearly all the features of what geographers call a hydraulic civilization but for the absence of a written language. Yet, in what is believed to be a relatively short period of time, Hohokam appears to have been either attacked by outsiders or abandoned by others who were once part of this magnificent cultural complex or living on its periphery. Either way, by the time Columbus arrived in the Caribbean, Hohokam was no more.

What happened? When the complex social organizational features of Hohokam are added to the physical features of these people and their place, understanding the rise and demise of the Hohokam society seems especially relevant to a twenty-first-century Southwest likely to face a water crisis. Knowledge of the Hohokam cultural complex is crucial today because many scientists forecast that Phoenix and much of the southwestern United States, from Southern California to New Mexico, will in the near future experience climate-change-related drought. And, in fact, it appears a major drought in the Southwest is already well underway and moving into its second decade of existence. To borrow the message "wisdom sits in places" from Keith Basso's book of that title, Hohokam reminds us that wisdom may indeed sit in places and involve an awareness of complexity that defies simplistic interpretations.

As an engineering feat, the Hohokam irrigation system was exceptional. However, Hohokam's historical and cultural importance exists in the fact that it exemplifies a case study in technology trumped by climate and societal organization—something the residents of Phoenix and Tucson might want to consider as mindless megadevelopment continues between and around these two desert cities. The canal system, started between 600 and 700 AD, reached its full development over the course of the next five hundred years. Consisting of hundreds of miles of channels running north and south from the Salt and Gila rivers, it was capable of irrigating tens of thousands of acres. The canals ranged from several to twenty-six meters wide and some were six meters deep. The system even featured a canal that extended twenty miles beyond its river source.

This system was not merely one of many crude ditches that transported water, but a carefully engineered network, as Jerry B. Howard detailed in "Hohokam Legacy: Desert Canals," in the Pueblo Grande Museum Profiles No. 12:

> As the amount of water traveling through the canal decreases through discharge onto fields, evaporation and seepage, the size of the channel carrying the water is reduced. By reducing the channel, the velocity of the water (the speed it travels through the channel) remained relatively constant and between two critical thresholds: if the water traveled too fast, it eroded the sides of the canal; if the water slowed down, particles of soil would settle out of the water, causing the canal to quickly "silt up," and require increased maintenance.[1]

By 1200 AD the Hohokam cultural complex would have struck anyone traveling through the area as not so much an oasis, but, given the strategic organization and sophisticated design of the canals, as a man-made marvel distinguished by its dramatic divergence from the surrounding landscape.

For those who insist on characterizing societies in the Americas before the arrival of Europeans as primitive—in other words, organizationally simple, subsistence societies—it is obvious they have little knowledge of Hohokam and her two contemporary North American cultural centers, Chaco Canyon and Cahokia. All three societies evidence a social complexity that continues to leave most archaeologists struggling to figure out exactly how to characterize them. But one feature of all three is indisputable: their physical construction required an incredible amount of human labor.

In the case of Hohokam, scholars today believe that no less than 1,200,000 cubic meters of soil were moved to create the canal system that covered an area of approximately 4,000 square miles. Keeping in mind that this earth was removed by hand with nonindustrial technology, Howard reported that it would have taken 25,000 person days to have completed the canal. The fact that this work required substantial labor and supporting food surpluses to facilitate such an undertaking is undeniable, even if the canals were a centuries-long, tedious work in progress.

Adding to the intrigue of the Hohokam legacy is the presence of large, elevated, rectangular platform mounds scattered throughout the villages. These were often three to ten feet in height, a hundred feet in length, and slightly less in width. The labor requirements to construct the platform mounds were substantial and indicate the availability of surplus agricultural products and labor. Their supposed function continues to stir disagreement among archaeologists today. But whether they were built for elite housing, as some have suggested, or for a religious and ceremonial integrative function, their existence makes clear that there was considerable complexity of social organization in the Hohokam heartland.

Further complicating the character of Hohokam culture was the presence of more than two hundred ball courts. These were built between 750 and 1250 AD and show clear evidence of a Mesoamerican influence. They pose serious questions about the social organizational and ideological features of the Hohokam peoples. The urge is to see Hohokam ball games as similar to those of the Maya and Aztecs, whose games took on a mythic, sacred, and even celestial character with implicit political functions. However, minus good ethnographic evidence, we have no way of knowing exactly what happened on the ball courts of Hohokam or why. More questions than answers remain about the kinds of social systems that actually held together and seemed to orchestrate this elaborate man-made physical cultural system through the course of its existence.

When one factors in the time and energy that went into the construction and maintenance of the canals and large platform mounds throughout Hohokam, not to mention the time spent watching and playing ball, the degree of statelike development may be questioned, but not the social complexity. Complexity in social organization should be expected in a desert society possessing such elaborate—some might say extravagant—physical cultural features. Yet, sociocultural complexity did not allow Hohokam to endure once the extreme flooding and drought of the 1200s hit the Salt and Gila river valleys.

In an excellent article, "Ancient Cultural Interplay of the American Southwest in the Mexican Northwest," authored by David R. Wilcox, Phil C. Wiegand, J. Scott Wood, and Jerry B. Howard and published in June of 2008 in the *Journal of the Southwest*, competing theories regarding Hohokam are examined in a larger regional context. The authors conclude that from an outside-looking-in perspective, all of the Salt River Valley was integrated into one political system.[2] While the precise social mechanism for this political integration remains unclear and open to interpretation, this much seems worth considering: water and control of it were the lifeblood of Hohokam.

The maintenance of power is often a complicated affair, especially when water is the material source of power in a desert environment. When water is no longer guaranteed or controllable, the maintenance and reproduction of power is tenuous and complicated. Drive the landscape of the desert Southwest today—from Los Angeles to Las Vegas, to Phoenix, to Tucson—and one will likely be impressed by the incredible development that has occurred in these places in just the last fifty years. When everything works, we take for granted the complexity of the infrastructure that allows our faucets to flow, the swimming pools to be filled, and our modern games to go on. Life is good—or so it seems.

Nowhere are the anthropocentric features of the modern American worldview and modern notions of history more obvious than in our inattentiveness regarding water, especially in the desert. Water, its presence and absence, will be the most obvious manifestation of our burning of the planet. The current prognosis for climate-change effects in the Southwest suggests that the water of the Colorado River will become much more valuable than it already is. With nearly all current climate models forecasting less water for the western United States, expect the scale of the twenty-first-century water wars to eclipse anything we saw in the range wars of the late nineteenth century.

This is hardly hyperbole. Read Lloyd Burton's *American Indian Water Rights and the Limits of Law* and check out the documentary film *Cadillac Desert*. The prospects for supporting the kind of desert metropolises we have built in the Southwest are dim. Sadly, the same can be said for the central plains irrigation-dependent agricultural systems, which, at current rates of drawdown or abstraction, are using water of the Ogallala Aquifer at a rate ten times faster than they can be replenished. Depending on where one lives, this means there is the possibility of no aquifer water within a few decades.

The wisdom that resides in the desert Southwest, and that is centered today, ironically, in Phoenix, Arizona, on land once inhabited by the Hohokam, might well be that large human settlements are unsustainable in such environments. If, as Wilcox and his coauthors imply, some of the persons once a part of the Hohokam cultural complex simply walked away when life became too difficult, in spite of the complex systems established to support them, new questions emerge: Where will the people of the large urban center of the Southwest now walk to? Where will they go? These are good questions for those willing to accept that life in a nature-culture nexus often requires more than ingenuity. It requires indigenuity: wisdom residing even in the demise of Hohokam.

Present: The Menominee—The Forest Keepers

The Menominee Nation is an excellent example of the deep spatial knowledge that embodies the symbiotic nature-culture nexus from which indigenuity emerges. The Menominee mark their time in the woodland region of the landscape now called Wisconsin as about ten thousand years. They call themselves the Kaeyas-Machatiwduk, or "Ancient

Ones," and today number about eight thousand members. Their long residency in the Northwoods has given them a keen awareness of the forest environs that gave them their identity. Indeed, the name *Menominee*, "people of the wild rice," was given to them by neighboring indigenous peoples because of their widespread use of wild rice.

Their story as a people is one of trials, tribulations, and, ultimately, resilience. During the twentieth century the Menominee developed a successful forestry program and wood-products manufacturing business. However, by midcentury, in part as a result of their economic success, the Menominee Nation was marked for termination. This was a devastating policy pursued by the federal government to eliminate the sovereign nation status of tribes and incorporate tribal nations into state jurisdictions. In 1961 the Menominee Nation ceased to exist, and the reservation lands (approximately two hundred thousand acres) became the seventy-second county in Wisconsin. A decade of social and cultural upheaval and economic chaos ensued, until 1973 when the Menominee land was successfully restored to reservation status and the Menominee people were once again recognized as a sovereign nation.

In spite of a recent history full of social disruption and turmoil, the Menominee have demonstrated a resilience that is in part an expression of their multigenerational deep spatial experiential body of knowledge complemented by scientific information and knowledge about the forest. The Menominee appreciate the forest in a way modern industrial foresters cannot, because unlike the spatial knowledge conveyed with the most sophisticated geographic information systems, they possess an experiential sense of place that tells them who they are as unique humans: the forest-keepers, Kaeyas-Machatiwduk, the Ancient Ones.

The *Menominee Tribal Enterprises: The Menominee Forest-Based Sustainable Development Tradition* by Maeqtekuahkihkiw Kew Kanāhwihtahquaq, "The Forest Keepers," states: "This bounty cannot be measured in financial terms alone, but must include a balance of environmental, economic, cultural, community, and spiritual values. Today celebrate the interconnectedness of the Creator's design so eloquently expressed by Mother Earth on the Menominee Indian Reservation." This deep spatial knowledge has given the Menominee the ability to apply some of the most modern technology and technical knowledge regarding forestry on their ancient indigenous ecological insights. As the Menominee state in this 1997 document: "The Tribe has learned from previous generations how a forest ecosystem interacts. We understand that the whole resource is needed to protect any part."[3]

Thomas Davis's book on Menominee forestry, *Sustaining the Forest, the People, and the Spirit*, documents the integrated complexity of Menominee culture and reached the conclusion that, after one hundred fifty years, "what the Menominee have achieved with their forest has the feel of what scholars and environmentalists mean by sustainable development."[4]

Ronald L. Trosper, professor and director of the Native American forestry program at Northern Arizona University and member of the Confederated Salish and Kootenai Tribes of the Flathead Indian Reservation in Montana, has examined the Menominee and their relationship to the forest and found three ancient indigenous features of their worldview that explain why, in many respects, they were doing sustainable forestry before there was "sustainable forestry" in Euro-American forestry enterprises. First, according to the Menominee creation story, man and woman were animals before they became humans. These persons established the Menominee clan system of social organization that consists of animal identities and totems that symbolically remind the Menominee to see themselves as a part of nature, not separate from the natural world. Their interaction with the natural environment of the forest is best understood as one among relatives, not as humans extracting resources.

Second, the Menominee understand that, like humans, the nonhuman or other-than-human features or persons, as many indigenous languages signify them, possess an active spirit that possesses power that must be respected. In this sense, successful living in a community constituted of other-than-human relatives requires their active cooperation and participation in order for humankind to live well. As a result, a host of practical activities must be undertaken to ensure that the power of the forest is not taken for granted. Often these practical activities include prayer and ceremony in many indigenous traditions. Not surprisingly, *The Menominee Forest-Based Sustainable Development Tradition* begins: "It is tradition among the Menominee People to open an event with a message of thanksgiving to the Great Spirit. Today we ask for a clear understanding and appreciation of the great bounty we have inherited from our ancestors. We ask for the wisdom to recognize our responsibilities as stewards of today's resources and to ensure their safekeeping for future generations."[5]

The third feature of the Menominee worldview Trosper found was "a belief that land belonged to the entire tribe, and that protecting the land was the duty of everyone."[6] The idea of communal possession of the land as well as a communal responsibility with regard to the land complements the first two ideas. In spite of a headlong attempt by the US government to undermine this value, it remains deeply held and widely shared among American Indians and Alaska Natives.

Menominee forestry practices serve to debunk the stereotypes, even today, that some of the "friends" of the Indians want to hold on to regarding use of modern technology. Menominee forestry practices demonstrate that all technology need not be rejected to live indigenously. Rather, their adoption and use of modern techniques and tools demonstrates that adoption of specific technologies ought not be reduced to an economic production calculation, but an inquiry into how such technologies promote key features of the Menominee worldview and values: humakind's connectedness and relatedness to the natural world, the fundamentally spiritual character of the natural world, and a deep sense of communal possession and responsibility for the land.

The thanksgiving passage quoted earlier embodies another widely shared indigenous idea the Menominee seem to embrace: a seven-generations way of thinking about one's community and responsibilities. Almost two thousand miles west of the Menominee forests, Hereditary Chief Edward Moody of the Nuxalk Nation, on the central coast of what is now known as British Columbia, Canada, expressed seven-generations thinking to the British Columbia Supreme Court on Februrary 12, 1999, in defense of an ancient rain forest valley known as Ista in the Great Bear Rainforest of British Columbia this way: "We must protect the forests for our children, grandchildren, and children yet to be born. We must protect the forests for those who can't speak for themselves such as the birds, animals, fish, and trees."[7]

Vine Deloria Jr. once shared with me a version of seven-generations thinking an elder explained to him: Each one of us is the seventh generation—at the center of life, preceded by three generations and followed by three generations. Our decisions, Deloria related, should take into account the knowledge of our ancestors—an intellectual and spiritual inheritance—and the responsibilities we have for our children and future generations, a sort of intellectual and spiritual trusteeship. The Menominee thanksgiving passage acknowledges their inheritance, recognizes their responsibilities today, and asks for wisdom to ensure the safekeeping of today's resources for future generations. As such, their thanksgiving constitutes a statement of seven-generations thinking, and like Chief Moody's affirmation of our responsibilities for those "who can't speak for themselves," the Menominee sustainable forestry practices constitute precisely this affirmation.

None of this is to say that problems are nonexistent on the Menominee Reservation. As with many reservations, the legacy of misguided federal Indian policies, and in their case the Policy of Termination, has left an intergenerational transmission of trauma that manifests itself in social dysfunction. Rather, the point is that while they are keepers of the forest, the land—their homeland—has kept them.

Future: Wind Power on the Plains

Among all the clans of the Euchee people, the Wind clan stands out among those of the nonanimal clan totems. Given the fact that the Euchee homelands were in the southeastern United States before the infamous Trail of Tears, one might easily conclude after a still, hot midsummer day why the Euchee recognized the wind as so important among their relatives: the breeze was welcomed in our arbors, our summer dwellings, for living within fixed walls would have been oppressive. Although the ability to catch a breeze is again factoring into some of the most innovative green housing designs today, few Americans realize that one of the largest reservoirs of untapped energy in North America exists in the winds blowing across the reservation lands of the central and northern plains.

Centered in the northern plains states of North Dakota, South Dakota, and Nebraska, the Intertribal Council on Utility Policy (ICOUP) was created in 1994 to provide a forum on utility issues facing the tribes of those states. Current tribal membership consists of the Cheyenne River Sioux; Flandreau Santee Sioux; Lower Brule Sioux; Mandan, Hidatsa, and Arikara; Omaha; Rosebud Sioux; Sisseton Sioux; Spirit Lake; and the Pine Ridge and Standing Rock Sioux tribes.

If the Hohokam cultural complex allows us to look to the past for life-enhancing knowledges and the Menominee sustainable forestry plan demonstrates what has been done with ecological insight, then the ICOUP allows us to envision a relationship to the wind that could benefit tribal nations, the larger US society, and, most importantly, Mother Earth in the near future. Pat Spears, president of ICOUP, states the vision clearly:

> The Tribes in the Northern Plains have a huge wind resource, one of the best on the planet. It has the potential to provide clean renewable energy for Tribal use and sustainable economic development, as well as for export to large population centers in the Western and Midwestern regions. Wind energy from Tribal lands alone can meet at least one-third of the nation's energy needs. Wind energy has the greatest potential to restore our economies. With more than half of our population under the age of 20, wind energy development can provide skilled technical employment for our youth.[7]

Imagine creating a renewable energy and revenue stream that would not entail the environmental degradation that epitomizes coal-burning facilities. In fact, some American Indians already have that vision. Tex Hall, past president of the National Congress of American Indians and chairman of the Mandan, Hidatsa, and Arikara nations likes to point out that his tribe has a wind-energy surplus of about 1.7 million percent, or seventeen thousand times more wind power than they can use on their Fort Berthold reservation. In 2004 the National Renewable Energy Laboratory estimated tribal lands could produce 14 percent of the total US electricity generated. To put that in perspective, imagine every major city on the Great Lakes having its electricity needs met by tribal wind-energy utilities and you get the picture—one minus acid rain, too. With some help from Congress, American Indian nations could aid the United States' efforts to dramatically reduce its carbon footprint and increase its energy security. Although the federal government has established the Renewable Energy Production Incentive, the Clean Renewable Energy Bonds, and the production tax credit (PTC) to serve as incentives for renewable-energy development, the first two have attracted little tribal participation, and the PTC, the most direct and user-friendly of the three incentives, cannot by law benefit tribally owned renewable-energy enterprises. In fact, as currently written, the PTC incentive for non-Native investment in wind energy constitutes a disincentive for American Indian wind-energy development. The PTC allows private investors to receive tax credits to offset private investors' costs. However, the tax-exempt status of American Indian tribal nations means that tribes receive no such investor incentive to offset costs unless they sell the ownership of their wind-energy projects to private investors. The result is counterproductive to tribal ownership and development of their tribally owned renewable energy economies. The Western Governors' Association and the National Congress of American Indians have both endorsed a change in the law to "partnership sharing," which would allow tribes to share their unused PTCs with private investment partners, thereby creating an incentive for tribally owned wind-energy projects and private investor partnerships. By allowing tribal joint ventures in wind energy to share unused PTCs with private partners, the United States might reduce their role in climate burning and encourage a sustainable form of economic development that has thus far eluded too many tribes.

In 2007 the ICOUP won one of the first World Clean Energy awards at the Faktor 4 Festival in Basel, Switzerland, for their Intertribal Environmental Justice Wind Demonstration Project. From an indigenous perspective, the issue of continued dependence on fossil-fueled energy technologies constitutes an environmental injustice in the deepest sense. It is impossible to continue using such non-renewable and climate-burning energies without creating injustices throughout human societies and throughout the life system of Mother Earth. Tribal wind energy can play a significant role in America's energy future if economic disincentives are removed and new obstacles are not placed in the way. While the ICOUP has primarily focused on macro-level wind-energy generation, they also recognize the importance of micro-wind-turbine technology. Improved technology in micro-wind-turbine design now allows owners of medium-sized houses in moderate wind environments who want to live off the grid to do so. For those who want a landscape without power lines and rows of macro-wind-energy turbines, the continued improvement of micro-turbines and their increasingly lower cost makes micro-wind-energy generation more attractive.

Can the wind be exploited? I do not know, but I trust peoples with traditions steeped in respect for Mother Earth's gifts, like the wind, to maintain good relations with this powerful gift. The ICOUP has a vision, and it is time to see how widely shared this vision is, and if the powers, place, and indigenous peoples of the northern plains want to enact this vision. We may not need a weatherman to know which way the wind blows, but we do need persons and peoples with vision to exercise an indigenuity that extends our ancient relationship to the wind in new ways.

WHAT WE CAN LEARN

The examples of the Hohokam, the Menominee, and the tribal nations of the northern plains participating in the ICOUP remind us that the past, present, and future offer themselves not so much as a universal unfolding of human history, but as unique space and time experiences emergent from our inevitable human involvement in a nature-culture nexus. If we are to successfully address the incredible changes the carbon-burning economies of the planet have set in motion, we must begin to think about what the past, present, and future embody, right here, right now, in particular places on the face of our Mother Earth. In order to not merely survive, but thrive in a period requiring human adaptation to dramatic climate changes, humankind must recognize that indigenous peoples possess rich experiential positioning systems that might inform choices we ought to make in order to live sustainably so we can literally and figuratively position ourselves to build systems of life enhancement.

Insight, knowledges, and sometimes even wisdom will come to those who begin to pay attention to their lives as they are situated daily in a nature-culture nexus. At their deepest level, indigenous knowledges remind us that we can never literally go back—a linear pattern of thought par excellence—to the world we used to live in. However, even with dramatic climate changes, as indigenous traditions and lifeways have demonstrated and continue to demonstrate, we can move ourselves outside the boxes that enclose our physical selves and imprison our minds and spirits to find a world we can live in.

Indigenous people made mistakes, miscalculations, and took more than a few missteps: Hohokam, Cahokia, and Chaco Canyon suggest as much. Indigenous folks in the past moved on, and, sadly, today some will be forced to move, but many of us will simply have to find better ways to live where we are. In the place of deterministic views of either the environmental or technological varieties regarding who we are, let us exercise the bio-mimicry advocated by Black Elk when he observed that his people of the Great Plains found ways to express their lives in circles, like the circular and cyclical life activities and processes of the living world that surrounds us.

CHAPTER SIX

Realizing Our Human Selves in the Nature-Culture Nexus

The nature-culture nexus is the unique interaction between a people and place. It embodies the existential feature of our oldest tribal traditions and identities as peoples. Improvement of the Earth's well-being and ours will be found in these oldest living indigenous expressions and the knowledges embedded in our native languages and tribal traditions. These knowledges offer a stark contrast to the unrealistic delusions sold to consumers around the globe—delusions of wealth, comfort, convenience, and control built on carbon-based technologies that are nearly all burned up. The Earth can no longer support cultures built on the narcissistic delusion that carbon-based lifeways in modern strip-malled (or -mauled) suburbia can continue with only some minor technological innovation.

Two of the most articulate and learned forecasters regarding the end-of-oil age we have now entered are respected geoscientists and former Shell Oil employees M. King Hubbert and Kenneth S. Deffeyes. Read Hubbert's and Deffeyes's work and you will see why the leading Fortune 500 corporations are taking climate change seriously. Sure, there is much that we do not know, and this will be frustrating for many in a society that wants knowledge and satisfaction immediately, but what we do know is more than enough to make the hair on the back of your neck stand up. As the Intergovernmental Panel on Climate Change's recently released report "Impacts, Adaptation, and Vulnerability" documents, we have clear empirical evidence that humankind is changing the biosphere of our planet in a manner that will endanger and diminish life on Earth.

We will need a lot of technological innovation and indigenuity, something radically different than the carbon-based technology to which we are currently addicted. Most importantly, we will have to change the way we live and think.

It seems trivial at one level, yet absolutely necessary at another, to remind modern humankind that the reason American Indians were and remain, to a surprising extent, culturally diverse signals the importance of the nature-culture nexus. From our most defining and expressive ceremonies to our centuries-old material cultures and, in the broadest sense, lifeways, it is hard to mistake the cultural traditions of a Seminole for a Lummi or a Menominee once one learns the locations of each of these peoples' long-standing homelands. No one would expect peoples coming from such diverse landscapes and environments as the wetlands of south Florida, the northwest coast of the United States, or the forest areas surrounding the Great Lakes to have dressed the same way, eaten the same foods, and lived in the same kinds of dwellings.

Within indigenous traditions, even our most sacred ceremonies, many still ongoing, speak to the importance of recognizing the nature-culture nexus. Are you surprised that the people of the northwest coast ceremonially honor the salmon and the whale? Why do the indigenous people of the Great Plains honor the bison? Would you expect the so-called Sioux peoples of the northern plains to have a salmon ceremony? Why do the tribes of the deep coastal South and southeastern United States have alligator clans, while the Menominee, Abanaki, and Passamaquoddy do not?

The fact that today the mainstream American culture is increasingly homogenized is indicative of the degree to which the way most Americans, in this modern, or, if you choose, postmodern, society, live with diminished and shallow connections to the places where they live.

Indigenous realism encourages humankind to reexamine ancient knowledges that were emergent from our ancestors' interaction with a place and, more importantly, to carefully examine useful knowledges that lay dormant but ready to emerge in the diverse ecosystems and landscapes surrounding us. In spite of the heavy footprints humankind has left on our planet, it may be but another illustration of a modern-civilization-inspired arrogance to think that we have so disrupted life on Mother Earth that there is nothing left for nature to teach us.

To the contrary, if we can instill an attentiveness to what I once heard described by an elder at an intertribal geographic information systems meeting as the natural LAW—respect for the land, air, and water—on which humankind and the biology of the planet depend, then there is much to be learned. This indigenous formulation of the natural law for life on the planet represents what we so often forgot in our technology-dominated and -shaped "world": real, tangible places and people inhabit a living planet more extensive and complex than the satellite images we seem to obsessively want to fix our gaze upon convey. The screens on televisions, computers, phones, and a host of media players we compulsively want at our disposal may be useful, but they have unintended consequences if we rely too heavily on them for our knowledge of the world. Too often we forget that the image produced by the camera eye gives us a greatly limited perspective of what is going on in the space-time beyond the screen.

In order to avoid misunderstanding, it must be explicitly stated that what is here called *indigenous realism* certainly acknowledges the colonial-imposed discontinuity, disruption, displacement, and attempted dissolution of all that made and continues to make us indigenous and tribal peoples desiring to live beyond the control of colonial institutions. Indigenous realism acknowledges this five-centuries-old frontal attack and recognizes the necessity of fighting "the Man" to save "the Indian," as several of my students have so aptly put this struggle, thereby placing Captain Richard Henry Pratt's credo firmly on its head. However, indigenous realism refuses to be placed in an exclusively negative critique of or reactive mode to colonial institutions infatuated with human-centered design and technique.

Indigenous realism places the most important life challenges Native peoples face—and, for that matter, those that all of humankind face—on common ground, literally and figuratively. It affirms patterns and processes beyond our own human making—patterns residing in ancient environs, such as wetlands, mountain ranges, prairies, and coastal estuaries and seascapes, and processes emerging in these environs, some of relatively short duration and some extending far beyond directly observable human time frames, such as the processes embodied in the hydrologic cycle, nutrient cycling, and the rock cycle, to name a few.

The great fallacy of Western thought was to think of the "human condition" as exclusively a condition defined by and about ourselves—a fallacy of omission engendered by a historical amnesia perpetuated by our increased habitation in manufactured spaces, places, and environments.

Today—right here, right now—indigenous realism, in many respects, encourages us to ask questions about how we should live. Our human ancestors found this unnecessary and even unimaginable because of the richness of community and shared experience they found themselves within. The questions are neither scholastic (in other words, dry academic fodder) or touchy-feely New Age ideology. They are practical questions about the means and consequences of extending the political and moral sphere of our "human condition" to life beyond our human selves—to extend our notion of community to our natural relatives that make possible and constitute the ecosystems in which we reside. The great humanistic Renaissance declaration—Man: the measure of all things!—has shown itself wanting.

American Indian and Alaska Native traditions have, with a few notable distinctions, the great advantage of never being seduced by self-assessed power and knowledge. Many North American indigenous traditions apparently recognized the possibility of a natural law minus a human-centered, anthropocentric scheme.

Indigenous natural law ought to be the foundation of an elementary school ecology lesson in every science curriculum around the world. For those of us living in the most modern of societies, it is impossible to remember something we never knew. Many of us, especially the baby-boomer generation, have lived in environments so heavily marked by human design and technology that our sense of place is predominantly informed by interiors and urban landscapes so manufactured it is difficult to extract positive natural lessons from such places.

Urban and suburban interiors and landscapes are so artificial it seems difficult to learn lessons other than the dramatic ones we encounter in their negative actualities and statements. We learn it is foolish to build cities and homes on river floodplains, most ocean coastlines, back-filled marshes and wetlands, and the sides of many beautiful but unstable hillsides. In a world where people are increasingly connected by electronic media in ways that only a generation ago were barely imaginable, it is easy to forget that, collectively, our human ancestors share a vastly longer and deeper history as tribal members than as citizens of modern nation-states.

It is a mistake to think that I am advocating a simple geographical or environmental determinism, a relationship where culture is unilaterally shaped by the geological, ecological, and climatological features of a place. The indigenization process facilitated through the concept of the nature-culture nexus is an attempt to overcome what John Dewey called the miseducative features of the Western dualism, or invidious distinction between nature and culture. It should now be clear that, in light of the scale of climate-change issues brought about by global burning, we can no longer debate issues of human and life sustainability, in general, in the philosophical context of a nature-versus-culture logic.

In fact, the impossible position of either/or reductionism is indicative of the existential features of the human condition. This situation—this nexus of relations—that Dewey, a non-Native philosopher, and Vine Deloria Jr., an American Indian philosopher, addressed throughout their writings suggests that understanding is more important than knowledge as truth, or knowledge as certainty, for humankind. The frame of reference, the measuring stick for human well-being, can only nominally be declared objective, for we have no choice but to acknowledge what sociologist Anthony Giddens calls our "double involvement" in the world: we are simultaneously products of and producers of the world in which we live.

The nature-culture nexus in which we are immersed is existential fact—the closest thing we can call objective fact. However, this fact has not and cannot yield a consensus among humankind regarding how we should live. The nature-culture nexus cannot do so, so long as we approach the question of how we should live from the either/or perspectives of culture versus nature, subjective versus objective, spiritual versus material, and any other of the obvious long-standing Western dichotomies. Nor can we, given the complexity of this planet's biosphere, expect to find a universal cultural expression or formulation for how humankind can live well on the planet.

There is no formula for life. Life is too complex, too rich, for simple parsimonious mathematical or formal logical expression. The basic physical conditions, including chemical and biological, for our human existence can be clearly stated and described. But even our most ancient philosophers have noted that living for most of our kind goes beyond merely existing and surviving. We struggle for existence when we must, but as psychology and numerous other fields of human inquiry confirm, humankind endeavors to find in their living—or, more accurately, through our life activities—ways to enhance our experience.

How should we live? Indigenous wisdom suggests it depends. It makes all the difference in the world, so to speak, *where* one lives in the diverse biosphere of Mother Earth when addressing the practical choices human beings make about how to live well. The conditions in which we find life, even our own human life, vary widely. The environments through which humankind moves and lives are diverse, thus any generalization or abstract expression or formula regarding life sustainability must accommodate the diversity of places humankind inhabits.

Humankind has created places that are unsustainable and impoverishing life. Our ability to acknowledge and act responsibly in this situation—this inconvenient truth, as Al Gore calls it—may tell us much about our place on the Earth. As the science writer David Quammen reported in *Harper's Magazine* in October of 1999, the Earth is becoming a planet of weeds. In the place of rich, biologically diverse environments, we increasingly find environments taken over by weeds, invasive species that push out native species. In the face of an incredible loss of biological diversity and a global climate change that will affect every geographic region on the Earth, it is reasonable to ask if humankind is a weed species. During the last five hundred years, it seems that every environment we humans moved into experienced a decline in biological diversity.

There is good news and bad news in such an assessment. The good news is this assessment forgets that when European nations began their colonial enterprises, they arrived on shores where human societies often lived within rich biological diversity. In short, the "we" that moved across the globe was not humankind in general, but, as Kirkpatrick Sale demonstrated in *The Conquest of Paradise*, people fully imbued with the values of modern Western civilization and representing prototypical European nation-states. The bad news is that at the beginning of the twenty-first century, humankind living in modern industrial and postindustrial societies cannot even fathom the good news embodied in this fact.

The problem we face today is that a large number of humankind on the planet took an incredible misstep during the course of the past few centuries. They built industrial societies that forgot the big picture of life on the planet—a picture that recognizes that we members of the human species are but one small part of life on our Mother Earth. However, there is hope for the future. Hope resides in examining tribal lifeways and extracting insights that can be used today with new knowledges and technologies acquired. Today we need leaders in our tribal nations and the larger nation states of this planet with vision informed by indigenous realism and indigenuity. We need leaders in all areas of our social lives who are willing to draw on the experiential knowledge embodied in the nature-culture nexus of peoples deeply connected to places.

Many political leaders throughout Indian Country and around the world continue to speak of sovereignty, self-determination, economic development, and occasionally even democracy. As important as these topics are in the everyday lives of humankind, in the big picture of life on the planet, such talk is beginning to appear meaningless unless explicitly related to the climate changes we are observing. Regardless of whether one lives in the polar and circumpolar regions, the Great Plains, the Gulf or northwest coast, the desert Southwest or New England, if one is paying attention, the changes in ecosystems, weather events, and the frequency and intensity of wild-fires are good reasons to get concerned about the role of what should honestly be called global burning in all of the above regions.

GLOBAL WARMING: HEATING OR BURNING?

Dr. James Lovelock, the father of modern Gaia theory, suggests the climate change and numerous indices of such change that scientists are now recording require us to think in terms of climate heating as opposed to warming. I have concluded that *global burning* is the most realistic desig-nation we can give to the climate-change phenomenon. This past summer, at a local copy center, I bumped into a University of Kansas colleague, sociologist David Smith. We exchanged greetings, and in passing I told him I was working on climate-change and global-warming issues. I immediately corrected myself and said *global-heating* issues. He quickly responded, following the logic of my correction, and suggested with ironic humor, "I think you mean *global-burning* issues." As I have thought more and more about the driving force behind climate change, I realized Smith was correct in his assessment.

From an indigenous cultural standpoint, I realized we must go one step further than Lovelock and name the complex phenomenon that the Earth-systems scientist might see as warming and the scientist with an eye to human-scale issues might see as heating, for what it represents in the most complete and fundamental sense: global burning. The issue scientists, economists, and a good number of people who live and work on the land and waters of our planet are presently documenting should be called global burning for three reasons.

First, we should be honest about the primary source of the heating we are observing. The human burning of fossil fuels is producing the climate changes we can now clearly document. We are literally heating up the Earth by burning up the fossil-fuel reserves of the Earth. Although studies of carbon dioxide sequestration may be necessary, the most direct way of addressing our current situation is to find ways to stop burning fossil fuels. The benefit of calling the climate change we are observing global burning is that this name encourages us to remember the primary source of the situation in which we find ourselves.

Second, while climatologists and Earth-systems scientists are correct in their geologic timescale to describe the current climate change as warming, from a very human standpoint what people are experiencing is starting to feel like burning. The Rapid City, South Dakota, airport recorded fifteen days above 100°F in 2006.[1] Six South Dakota locations set new all-time-high temperatures, with the hottest temperature reaching 120°F in Usta, South Dakota.[2]

Finally, burning may be the best metaphor for the friction that is beginning to manifest itself among the socioeconomic institutions of human societies as a result of climate heating. In the already smoldering areas of social justice, the social combustion that will be ignited as a result of global heating may well result in the collapse of many already dysfunctional social institutions around the planet. All people living in the midst of the United States, including American Indians and Alaska Natives, should not underestimate the extent to which the relative socioeconomic poverty experienced by many in this land can obscure the absolute poverty so prevalent throughout much of the world.

The gap between the rich and poor is growing around the world, but growing the fastest in this once-called "land of plenty": the United States. This economic gap, to say nothing of the spiritual poverty such a gap produces for all involved, will be exacerbated by climate change. Our climate in the physical science and social senses will, without substantive changes in the material cultures of the most powerful societies in the world, erupt into a social conflagration unparalleled in modern history. Our climate, in the broadest sense, is burning.

In order to move from the remediation models of dealing with the consequences of the human activity that is responsible for the climate change currently underway, humankind must take radical steps to realize a truly conservative and humble public policy that will ensure our children and grandchildren will not suffer from our inattentiveness to what is going on in "our own backyards," as my friend and colleague Margaret Hiza Redsteer, of the US Geological Survey, says. We must reconstitute, revitalize, and, for many people on the planet, reimagine what it means to live in a homeland—a homeland not in any nationalistic, political, or ideological sense, but a land one calls home by virtue of an intimate nature-culture nexus. Fortunately, we have peoples on the planet today who still know what it means to have a homeland, peoples who possess a cultural tribal identity that is emergent from the land and water where they live.

CHAPTER SEVEN

After Progress: A Reexamination of Traditional Technologies

Those possessing the Western, forward-looking gaze of progress, the linear temporal view of progressive world history, often forfeit insights that might be gained from an examination of technologies once used by our ancestors—and in a few places still used by tribal peoples today. The exploration of new knowledge and technologies must not overlook the knowledge and technologies that reside in tribal ways of living. Part of this prejudice can be seen in the knee-jerk response one often hears to suggestions to reexamine tribal knowledges and technologies: "Oh, so you want us to all go back and live in teepees and hunt bison."

Such a response is indicative of the shallow criticisms of proposals to look carefully at older knowledges, ways of living, and technologies in the context of their environments. Never mind that the American bison (*Bison bison*) that was the source of the teepee cover was nearly exterminated in the name of progress and civilization. Although population numbers vary, somewhere between forty and seventy million bison roamed the landscapes of North America around 1600 AD. Even as late as May of 1871, Colonel Richard Irving Dodge in his *Plains of the Great West and Their Inhabitants* recounted seeing a herd twenty-five miles wide along the Arkansas River on a trip from old Fort Zara to Fort Larned. But by 1900 less than a thousand bison lived on the landscapes of North America, with the greatest diminution of these magnificent herd animals occurring between 1830 and 1875 at a rate of two hundred thousand deaths a year as they were wantonly massacred for the sake of, above all else, civilization and progress.

No one is suggesting we go back and live in the past. That place, that landscape, does not exist anymore. The linear thinking associated with this objection demonstrates the extent to which such historical thinking operates in a largely abstract dimension of time. Our human lives and those of the planetary life system are but one small part of existence in space-time. The unique character of our historical situation is not an either/or proposition with respect to space and time. However, as I have suggested earlier, one way to indigenize our thinking about history is to grant space and place at least as much significance as time.

Life is, above all, an ongoing process, and a complex one at that. I reject the usefulness of the simplistic formulations of moving backward or forward along some abstract ideological notion of a universal history. We might do well to ask ourselves how residing in places might foster life enhancement—not so much making places our own, but allowing places to give us homes.

We must be absolutely clear about this: human societies cannot go back to the past, nor can we go to the future along any projected timelines informed by traditional or progressive ideological phantasms. However, we can, if attentive, live in what the American pragmatist John Dewey suggested was a coextensive present with both the past and the future. If American society will take Native cultures seriously, we can examine how indigenous tribal cultures, unlike the increasingly homogenous global consumer culture, maintain a tangible and meaningful connection between where a people live and how they live. The result will be useful knowledge about how living within a biosphere with diverse landscapes and environments requires cultures emergent from these environments.

Three areas of research—housing, food, and planning and assessment models—should be immediately undertaken to yield positive results for Mother Earth. The exciting thing about such an agenda is that it requires people- and place-specific investigations. The brief sketch that follows is merely suggestive of substantive research areas ripe for development.

LIFEWAY ISSUES: DWELLINGS, FOOD, AND DECISION-MAKING

Indigenous Dwellings versus Spec Housing

The rectangular spec—ticky-tacky, little, and now not so little—houses that continue to be built across Indian Country and throughout the United States are not only ugly, but extremely wasteful from an energy perspective. They may represent better than any material artifact the current homogenization of our material culture. From a conceptual and spiritual standpoint, these unimaginative houses embody the boxlike categories that dominate the human mindscape today. It is clear when one drives through suburban sprawls and the increasing number of faux-rural two- to five-acre estates that scar the countryside within an hour's drive of many Midwestern cities that a cultural disregard for space and place exists in the United States, especially when one sees the conspicuous consumption these oversized, poorly built, upscale suburban houses represent.

The location and orientation of these houses typically show no regard for the broader landscape, solar, wind, and microclimate features of their environment. All of the above factors ought to inform the design of these houses. Architects and designers, especially Native ones, should explore the insights our ancestors possessed that enabled them to build dwellings that took full advantage of the climate, landscape, and material features of their homelands. Sustainability issues were foremost when our ancestors, collectively speaking, designed and built the pueblos of the desert Southwest, grass lodges of the southern plains, earth lodges along the Republican and Missouri rivers, and the teepees of the plains. They had knowledge about how to build dwellings that fit the landscape they dwelled within.

Again, no one is suggesting that we go back to building exactly what they did, the way they did. What I am suggesting is that there may be appropriate and sustainable indigenous design features we should take advantage of today. The Caddo and Wichita peoples of the southern plains built grass lodges with cedar frames for family dwellings and larger community ceremonial purposes. In a landscape dominated by grass prairies, the use of grass as a building material was a perfect example of indigenuity. These lodges were durable, easily repaired, and comfortable for most of the year. Grass lodges were both breathable and waterproof. They fit the landscape of the Caddo and Wichita peoples.

Today some in the Great Plains are building straw-bale houses. These dwellings are a good, but not perfect, fit for many places on the plains where wheat has replaced the tallgrass prairies. They require surprising little reinforcement and are adaptable to many exterior finishes.

The next step, then, is to look seriously at design features of the Caddo and Wichita grass lodges to see how we might use current materials technology and design and engineering knowledge to avoid merely building straw houses that emulate the spec boxes where modern humankind can hardly be said to dwell, but more accurately described as warehoused.

In order to support the design and material indigenuity embodied in grass lodges, it is time to seriously consider what restoration of native grasses and a large bison population to the Great Plains would look like. It has been twenty-two years since Frank and Deborah Popper suggested the re-creation of a "buffalo commons."[1] It is now time to offer American Indian iterations of the buffalo commons idea and concentrate on how humankind can fit into such a vision. Maybe we humans do not have to all leave. When the policy makers bemoan and protest the cost of reconstituting the Great Plains as a habitat for bison and humankind, we must remind them to compare such calculations to the cost of continuing the unsustainable agribusiness operations and modes of human habitation currently found there.

One additional comment on these grass-thatch indigenous dwellings is worth noting. While traveling in Eastern Europe during the summer of 2006 as part of a George Soros–funded International Higher Education Support program, the research group I was part of visited a small village in northern Slovenia where folks were restoring traditional dwellings to be used as homes once again. I noticed most had corrugated metal or tile roofs, though I suspected they had thatched roofs earlier in their existence. Our project leader, Dr. Irena Sumi, confirmed my suspicion and related a situation I had heard once before concerning the disappearance of thatched roofs in parts of rural England and Ireland. She explained that the craftsmen who did such beautiful and efficient work were literally a dying breed. However, she also explained that people who wanted such roofs today, which are now very expensive, often imported workers from other parts of Europe. Our landscapes and seascapes are changing literally and figuratively.

As one moves north on the Great Plains to the Republican, Loup, and Missouri rivers, another example of indigenous architecture is found. The earth lodges of the Pawnee, Arikara, Hidatsa, and Mandan, like the grass lodges of the southern plains, are the embodiment of a symbiotic nature-culture nexus emergent from the environment. These structures were suited for the quickly changing weather conditions of the midcontinent climate. Above all, they could withstand the winds, even the violent tornadoes of the central plains, the entrance of the notorious tornado alley. There are no accounts of tornadoes ever destroying an earth lodge, and this, in and of itself, speaks to their practicality.

The earth lodges, like the grass lodges, varied in size, with some along the Republican River now known to have been as large as fifty feet across, and easily accommodated an extended family of thirty to forty members. The earth lodges of each respective tribe expressed unique design features. Among the Pawnee and the Arikara, the entire layout and interior spaces of ceremonial lodges contained symbolic representations of the cosmos and the unique place of each of these peoples within the cosmos.

These lodges were strategically situated in distance and elevation far enough from the rivers so that people could live there a large part of the year yet take advantage of the rich alluvial soils along the rivers for their farming activities. I once heard Bea Medicine describe the cyclical farming techniques of the Sioux on the Standing Rock Reservation. I was struck by the fact that the Sioux and other Native peoples on the upper Missouri River, primarily teepee dwellers, took full advantage of the river's rhythms. They appreciated the flood cycles of the rivers, and they knew better than to set up their full camps on the river's floodplain. It was easy to sleep out near their garden plots and move back to the safety of the village camps when the rain threatened. Such knowledge seems obvious, and it was to people who lived with the rivers.

Today such knowledge has been displaced with the modern engineering mentality and its goal of controlling or managing rivers. In this sense, it seems the US Army Corps of Engineers never saw a river it could not dam(n). After experiencing two so-called five-hundred-year floods on the Missouri and Kansas rivers within a three-year period in the mid-1990s, I thought of the hundreds of millions of dollars of flood damage in the cities built by the settlers all along the Missouri River and could not help but think things would have been much different if the tribal nations of the Missouri River basin had been consulted regarding the location and development of those cities. It remains to be seen if the US Army Corps of Engineers has "discovered" that, especially when dealing with rivers, the illusion of the control of nature has a very high cost.

Nourishment

If one agrees we need to change our dwellings in order to live in a more life-enhancing manner, then when it comes to the relationship between food and lifeways the case is even easier to make. There is little evidence that earlier generations of indigenous peoples and nonindigenous persons in North America had the kind of lifestyle diseases that plague us today. The irony of our situation is that while modern medicine, with its wedding of biology and chemistry, has extended life expectancy for everyone in the United States, albeit for some more than others, we now live longer to face a host of diseases that are not pathogen borne, but lifestyle, or, more accurately, lifeway diseases.

This, too, may change, for the December 6, 2007, issue of *The New England Journal of Medicine* reported what many of us have already observed: we now have an epidemic of childhood obesity. Dr. Kirsten Bibbins-Domingo of the University of California at San Francisco believes teenagers in the United States today will experience dramatically higher rates of coronary heart disease as young middle-age adults between thirty-five and fifty years of age.[2] The World Health Organization (WHO) sees similar trends developing around the globe. The problem is simply a combination of what we eat and the way those of us residing in the midst of modern and highly urban nations are living. According to the WHO, two factors stand out in explaining this obesity epidemic: the increasing lack of physical work and the consumption of commercial and fast foods high in fat and sugar, but low in vitamins, minerals, and other micronutrients.

While children are the most compelling victims of this epidemic because of their innocence, the guilty, so to speak, their parents and grandparents, are not exempt from this deadly lifestyle phenomenon either. Far too many Americans are overweight. The obesity epidemic is particularly dangerous because it is related to the onset of diabetes, high blood pressure, and coronary heart disease.

The highly processed food we eat today is a significant contributing factor to the obesity epidemic. The manufactured foods most Americans eat have lower nutritional value than what most of our indigenous ancestors ate only a century or two ago. Many living in the Unites States find it surprising to learn that, according to Slow Food International, we have decreased our food diversity by 93 percent during the last century in this land of plenty. We have one-tenth the choices of native foods our grand- and great-grandparents had. This radical diminution of food choice is largely attributable to the corporate monoculture farming practiced across the United States today.

We must move away from the agribusiness model of food production. Life on the planet cannot afford the cost of the factory-produced, -processed, and -packaged fast-food nation we have become. As Wes Jackson of The Land Institute outside Salina, Kansas, likes to point out, we have produced an agricultural system that is like a patient on an artificial life-support system undergoing intensive chemotherapy. Fortunately, some are recognizing that this agribusiness fast-food crisis is real. The slow food and local food movements represent some hope, especially as more and more people start growing and cooking their own food.

Nearly every elementary student in the United States today learns of the importance of what the Haudenosaunee, or Iroquois, called the "three sisters"—corn, beans, and squash—in indigenous American agriculture. Among all the valuable items transferred to Europe, none may have been as valuable as these protein-rich vegetables. In the big picture of fifteenth- and sixteenth-century Europe, the value of the transfer of wealth resulting from the extraction of gold and silver in the Americas may well have paled when compared to the transfer of health the three sisters and numerous other indigenous American foods and farming techniques represented to a European landscape beset by famine and disease.

With respect to our carnivorous appetites, we see the undeniable benefits of eating grassland bison, as many of our indigenous North Americans did, as opposed to feedlot-fattened cattle. Bison provide much leaner meat than manufactured beef does, if left on the prairie and kept out of the feedlots. No matter where we go on this continent, we find that tribal people knew how to exist on foods native to their environment, including wild game, fish, bison, corn, and wild rice. We should look very carefully at what modern nutrition science is telling us about contemporary diets. Where foods are viewed first and foremost as economic commodities, it appears that what we receive is impoverishing life as opposed to enhancing life, especially life in a diverse ecological sense.

Unfortunately, knowledge does not translate automatically into life-enhancing action. Most schoolchildren today live on fast food, a highly processed and fattened diet of burgers and fries, than they do the local native foods and homegrown garden foods that benefited their ancestors, indigenous and nonindigenous alike. Fortunately, it only takes some imagination and indigenuity to restore a land and peoples to one where obesity, diabetes, high blood pressure, heart disease, and cancer might significantly decline.

Good places to explore why and how we might indigenize our diets are found in Devon Abbot Mihesua's book *Recovering Our Ancestors' Gardens: Indigenous Recipes and Guide to Diet and Fitness* and Gary Paul Nabhan's *Cultures of Habitat: On Nature, Culture, and Story* and *Coming Home to Eat: The Pleasures and Politics of Local Foods*. Each book encourages us to reconnect in tangible ways to the life that we can too often take for granted when shopping the aisles of supermarkets. Gardening, gathering, hunting, fishing, herding, cooking, going to our local farmers' markets, even grocery shopping, and ultimately how, where, and with whom we eat can be something that connects us to each other and places in profound ways. Especially for the inattentive, the unaware, and those who simply do not care, shopping at superstores and grocery stores does connect us in profound ways to our life relatives, distant places, processes, and powers: in fact, this is a substantial part of the problem we face. The relationships that we are part of can be exploitative and damaging to all our relatives (human and other-than-human), especially when we forget, mistake, or become inattentive to the sources of the food we so conveniently buy at our nearest supermarket outlet.

Slow food, local food, and social food (social nourishment) may give us what we most need today: nourishment for our bodies, spirits, and communities. The industrial-driven and now the information-technology-driven economic wealth of the United States has come at a very high price: our health. Examination of what indigenous peoples ate in the places where one today lives, before food became commodities, might help us solve some critical environmental problems.

The reality of our fast-food nation may tell us more about the extent of our modern social and spiritual impoverishment than we care to acknowledge, for the challenges to realizing a culture of nourishment are deeply embedded in our modern lifeways. The irony is not found in our modern penchant for convenience, but in the fact that we now acquiesce so casually to hurried and harried lives against which the values of convenience is measured.

Indigenous Assessment

Three primary points should be made with respect to indigenous models of assessment. As mentioned earlier, we must explore a seven-generations model of planning and assessment. Also, our assessment models must draw on what Rick Williams, executive director of the American Indian College Fund, calls our "natural intelligence." Finally, rather than what I have heard euphemistically referred to as the "keep-it-simple, stupid" model of assessment, I suggest we think about *relationships in complex harmony* when doing assessment—a RICH model of assessment.

Our ancestors had good sense—an experiential wisdom—that allowed them to always be mindful of the complex results of actions they took. Necessity required them to be attentive to the land and learn from it and all our living relatives, including plants and animals. The notion that in the life system of planet Earth we are all connected and related is hardly romantic. Rather, it is a fair representation of what constitutes an ancient indigenous realism. Indigenous realism converges quite closely with what many scientists, engineers, and mathematicians now identify as complex adaptive systems, systems wherein the current situations and conditions we face are understood to be the result of processes through which structures consisting of numerous interacting parts result in dynamic processes.

The growing recognition that much of reality is better understood as complex dynamic interactions and processes not reducible to simplistic and deterministic cause-and-effect logic is something inherent in many indigenous North American worldviews. Consequently, bringing Native thinkers into the field of environmental planning and environmental impact assessment may be particularly useful since they are predisposed to big-picture planning and assessment. Our ancestors were thinking out of the box long before it became a popular catchphrase of corporate trainers.

In the American Indian and Alaska Native traditions with which I am familiar, the evaluation of our present life and activities appears centered on an intergenerational assessment that evaluates our proper conduct in the here and now based on the knowledge and respect of previous generations as well as future generations. The concept of the seven generations within a number of tribal traditions is a good example of an indigenous assessment tool. Even accepting some tribal variations in how it is understood and used, the concept is particularly relevant to assessment.

Vine Deloria Jr. told me the notion of the seven generations, used in several American Indian tribal traditions, was explained to him by a Dakota Sioux elder as signifying that at all times and in every place each of us is a unique expression of the seventh generation of our families and, more broadly, our people. In our lives, each of us constitutes the seventh generation in the sense that our actions ought to represent what we learned from three previous generations: parents, grandparents, and great-grandparents, and simultaneously we must be mindful of how our present actions will influence the lives of three future generations: our children, grandchildren, and great-grandchildren. Each of us, in our respective places in the space-time of the universe we inhabit, constitute the seventh generation at the center of the three generations that came before us and the three generations that will come after us.

As the seventh generation, we are the existential center of life processes that embody nonlinear relationships and complex processes in which, to appropriate a term from sociological theory, we have what Anthony Giddens calls a "double involvement." Our double involvement in history means we are simultaneously shaped by history and shapers of the future history, not in some abstract linear idea of a universal history, but in phenomenal spaces and places on the Earth that possess power that ought to inform our conduct.

At a Council of Energy Resource Tribes conference several years ago, distinguished scientist and environmental visionary Amory Lovins suggested assessment science was still in its infancy. He was right with respect to individuals still operating within the dominant Western worldview, but wrong with respect to Native thinkers. As we look to new models of assessment, the incorporation of the nature-culture nexus idea will yield tremendous results. As new greener and essentially indigenous technologies are sought, their assessment should be measured as positive value on a scale developed in the context of the nature-culture nexus.

The implication of disconnecting technology from the big picture of our human experience is that we forget the unique lessons we learned about living well, or, as my Citizen Band Potawatomi colleague and friend George Godfrey would say, "living lightly on the land." Today the problem is that the measure of technological progress is often thought of as the extent to which humankind can control and mitigate the so-called forces of nature. I find it hard to imagine a more problematic and potentially dangerous idea. We must figure out a way to live *with* nature.

We ought to think of ecosystems and environments as our natural communities—full of our relatives. We must recognize a symbiotic relationship between nature and culture. Keep in mind that human tribal identities, and the largest part of all human cultures until very recently, were literally emergent from the complex systems, the environment and ecologies, where we lived. What did we learn—and what have many already forgotten—from this rich history?

First, we can prevent the destructive side of technology from overshadowing its constructive features by incorporating ideas and concepts like the nature-culture nexus in practices of evaluation and assessment. The dichotomy of nature versus culture is not only false, but in the big picture of life, useless. As suggested earlier, the ideas of civilization, progress, and the entire industrial revolution were fueled by this dichotomy. We must acknowledge that ultimately, the deeply embedded dichotomy of nature versus culture is a damaging and deadly one.

However, it is a mistake to think that technology is the enemy. Modern technologies are merely instruments whose value has been mismeasured. We now face the challenge of identifying technologies that have value beyond the exploitative narrow economic measures of profit. By looking at the convergences now emerging between Western science and technology and indigenous lifeway knowledges and practices, we can develop a richer and ultimately more realistic measure for the value of technology.

However, for these two multifaceted traditions to come together, indigenous peoples need to create places where this integration is respectful and honest. Hopefully, tribal colleges will become these places. But even in our tribal colleges, science is too often shaped by large federal-funding sources, which seem to have only a token interest in indigenous worldviews, knowledge, and wisdom. This is in many respects the crux of the problem: so long as the classical experimental methodologies of science are held as the touchstone for true knowledge, the knowledges Native peoples acquired through many generations of living with the land and sea are precluded from serious consideration.

This situation seems to be changing. Yet, it remains to be seen whether indigenously informed programs, projects, and research initiatives will receive funding parity with traditional Western scientific activities. Application of indigenous ideas such as the nature-culture nexus, the principle of planning for seven generations, and the design insights gained through examination of preindustrial tribal dwellings could help minimize the destructive consequences of technology because they consider the value of technology found within the big picture of life on this planet. By doing the hard work of constructing measurement scales for technology within the experiential totality of our human lives—in other words, the physical, emotional, spiritual, and intellectual layers of life—we can avoid the largely precise abstract measures of value used today. What we lose in precision is more than compensated for in the advantage gained in establishing values for technology within specific environments.

The experiential totality of the nature-culture nexus is located in the specific places, the spatial situations, of unique ecosystems and the environment where our tribes lived and some still live. Our tribal cultures and worldviews were emergent from the places where we lived—the places we called home. Humankind cannot continue to buy into the homogenized landscapes being sold to us without greatly impoverishing the rich expression of cultural diversity that has been, until very recently, as much a part of Mother Earth's natural history as her mountains and seas.

One crucial point needs to be emphasized here: our ancestors made mistakes throughout their history. Look at the incredible cultural developments found at Pueblo Grande, Cahokia, Chaco Canyon, the complex of southwestern cliff dwellings, and many of the mound complexes of the eastern and southeastern United States—the first four were abandoned centuries before 1492. Yes, we made mistakes, and like most attentive humans, we learned from them. There is a much thinner line between trial and error and formal experimentalism than many scientists are willing to admit. No peoples or cultures on this planet have a spotless record when it comes to making choices that were unsustainable.

Discussions about sustainability, appropriate technologies, and what F. Henry Lickers calls "natural systems thinking" would be greatly enhanced if we had a generation of Native scientists, engineers, and planners who understood the tools of science and technology and possessed the ability to evaluate this knowledge within the context of our tribal worldviews. I suspect we would not lose technologies, but we would instead avoid making the mistake of thinking of technologies as independent of unique places and peoples on the planet. Why few individuals make the connection between the declining biological and ecological diversity and the declining diversity of peoples and cultures on the planet should be obvious: they disconnect technology from the crucial survival issues of community, communication, and culture.

I was once asked to give a presentation at a conference of engineers. I thought *If I want to get their attention, I better give them a formula.* The point I wanted to convey was that the value of a technology should never be reduced to purely economic terms. So I initially came up with the T3C expression, where the ultimate value of technology was weighted according to its enhancement of the three Cs: community, communication, and culture.

I also emphasized the fact that any measurement scale of value for technology needs to fit the particular part of the Earth's life system where the technology will be used. Sometimes the obvious escapes us: several people listening to my presentation pointed out that the particular landscape or environment—the place one lives—where any such formulation must be made was absent in this expression of value. Consequently, a new equation, $3C/E = T$, was born. This idea or expression of value always recognizes the environment as the denominator. The value of technology is established as a function of the symbiotic relationship between environment and culture or, as I have called it throughout this work, the nature-culture nexus.

We, and more importantly, the balance of life on the planet, cannot afford our continued assessment of human activities with anthropocentric measurement scales. Mother Earth is suggesting, and increasingly scientists agree, that our human values should be found in activities of life enhancement, not merely our own, but in measures of life enhancement for our planet.

We must consider how our lives and the life of our planet might be better served by realizing that politics based on inalienable rights might be empty, indeed poverty stricken, without a necessary complementary recognition of our inalienable responsibilities.

ACKNOWLEDGING A POLITICS OF INALIENABLE RESPONSIBILITIES

A successful coupling of cultural diversity with ecological diversity in practical lifeways and worldviews invites indigenuity. Many who think it is too late to do anything in this human-created climate crisis are half right. Half

right because substantial changes, some already catastrophic, have been set in motion and are well underway
in many places across the planet, most notably the circumpolar arctic regions. Much damage has been done to
Mother Earth, and more is underway. However, the "too
late" thinkers are equally wrong. As key players in this
planet's life system, we are indeed participants in what is
happening—there is no way to now opt out of the situation
we have created. Doing nothing, doing something—both
have consequences.

For those who want to raise issues about inalienable
rights as we think about what we should or should not do,
it may be time to ask if we might now consider adopting
an indigenous political discourse and practice based on
inalienable responsibilities. We should encourage difficult discussions of our current situation but acknowledge
that our knowing of what will happen in the future must
always be incomplete. We must be honest about the diffi-
culty science faces in our current situation. Those wanting
neat formulae to predict how this catastrophe will unfold
will be dissatisfied. A single neat formula or set of such formulae cannot capture the complexity, especially the rate
of change at which our climate is burning up. The Earth's
atmosphere and its interaction with many variables in the
more extensive biosphere will shape what people in certain
places on the planet will experience and when.

We should not wring our hands about this situation,
but roll up our sleeves and get to work. Those who ratio-
nalize inaction as their right to believe it is either too late
or too early to act on what is happening with Mother Earth
should consider framing the question, as a good number

of American Indian elders have done, in terms of responsibilities as opposed rights. What we do know is that our human activities have played the defining role in the global burning and climate change we are currently experiencing. Our response to this knowledge will play a defining role in how much disruption to life will occur. Let us not merely issue an SOS to save ourselves, but respond to a Red Alert that encourages humankind to acknowledge our inalienable responsibilities to the life that surrounds us. We must ensure future generations will have good stories to tell and songs to sing about the legacy with which we left them to live.

In many American Indian traditions, the inalienable responsibilities we are born with require us to act, lest the Earth, our mother, and all of her children remember us as the people who forgot their relations and their relatives. Before humans get too preoccupied with the time we have left, or some calculation of what time it really is relative to climate changes driven by global burning, we must remember that we are trying to reconnect, in a deep spatial and spiritual sense, to the places where we live and the life systems that support us.

Realism and humility suggest humans alone cannot save the Earth, yet the power of indigenous knowledges resides in the recognition that indigenous knowledges are, as I have used the term throughout this book, fundamentally Earth knowledges. On the very last page of Deloria's classic work *God Is Red*, he asked who was ready to listen to the mountains, forests, and the entire balance of nature beyond our human selves. This Red Alert is a reminder of that four-decades-old question. I recommend that those interested in saving the planet from great losses of life start by listening to the Earth knowledges, the indigenous knowledges, American Indians and Alaska Natives possess regarding ways to live well in the diverse environments of Mother Earth.

A MODEST CONCLUSION

We Cannot Save Ourselves without Some Human Homeland Maturity

The presumptuous-sounding claim that the Earth can be saved through indigenous knowledges at first seems more than a little arrogant: it sounds, quite frankly, unindigenous. The idea of "saving the planet" with any knowledge, as understood in the context of the dominant Western worldview, will connote the idea that we humans are in control of the Earth. However, such an idea is foreign to most of the worldviews of the American Indian and Alaska Native peoples I have had the good fortune to work with during the last three decades. Humility, not hubris, is the personal characteristic most associated with our knowledge-bearers, faith-keepers, and wisdom-keepers in North American indigenous traditions, a humbleness that acknowledges how pitiful we humans are in the big picture of life on Earth. We need a lot of help to become competent, mature members of humankind and our larger, more extensive ecological kinship relations.

Yet, how can any member of the species that is responsible for the monumental destruction of so much life on the planet during the last two hundred years make any claim to saving the planet? To be honest, we, human-kind alone, cannot make such a claim. We will have to call on the help of our relatives. We must pay attention and look to the plants, the animals, the wind, the water, the Earth, and our most distant relative, the sun, to stop an imminent Earth catastrophe. For if nothing substantially changes in the so-called advanced societies and the emerging global civilization of this planet to mitigate the devastation now well underway, many lives will be lost in our ecological communities. It is precisely this help, from these, our other-than-human relatives, that indigenous thinkers are not embarrassed to call on.

Advanced societies, with their powerful rationality and technologies, evidence an adherence to a body of myths and romanticism that eclipses anything imagined in tribal worldviews and lifeways. Primary among the myths to which modern humankind faithfully adheres is the deep-seated notion that humankind constitutes the center of creation around which the rest of the world revolves. This position is held self-evident by our "apparent" control and manipulation of the natural world.

If romanticism denotes impracticality and unrealistic fantasy, can there be a more romantic myth than the idea that humankind can always rise above the forces of nature through our rationalities and application of technology? Contrast this self-important and, ultimately, destructive romantic myth to the cultures of tribal peoples who possess lifeways and worldviews emergent from the unique environments they call home or homelands.

Right now the planet requires that humankind listens to what indigenous peoples are saying. Indigenous peoples—those who take their instructions for living from the sacred powers of this creation, the environment, ecosystems, and climates—possess useful knowledge much needed today. Mother Earth has issued a Red Alert. Indigenous peoples, those exercising the most attentiveness, have been echoing this alert for a very long time.

In order to appreciate this alert, the prejudices and stereotypes that have kept people from paying attention to indigenous thinkers and their lifeways must be set aside. One of these prejudices is instructive: the idea that civilization results from the human control and manipulation of nature has had deadly consequences for life on our planet. Native peoples around the world can speak directly to this point. The same logic that established a war between nature and so-called civilized humankind too often continues to justify wars against Native peoples so they and their lands can be controlled.

Modern societies are too infatuated with the powerful technologies humankind produced to serve *our* ends of comfort, convenience, and the control of nature. Too many of our leaders unrealistically think humankind stands above and independent of the rest of the natural world. This misguided notion holds that humankind can always rise above the forces of nature through our rationalities and use of technology. This is wrong.

Fortunately, tribal elders possess worldviews and lifeways (including technologies) closely tied to the unique environments where they have lived. And many Native peoples continue to find their identities, cultures, in the broadest sense, and, most important, life lessons in the landscapes and seascapes that they call home. Their indigenous knowledge systems emerge from their long-standing relationships with natural environments: an active participation in a symbiotic nature-culture nexus. Their main message is that nature and culture cannot be divorced—that biological diversity and cultural diversity are inextricably connected.

The new National Museum of the American Indian (NMAI) curates and displays features of material tribal cultures that are the embodiment of technical expertise and symbolic meaning. It is full of examples of the integration of power and place and peoples emergent from the constant nexus of nature and culture. The NMAI celebrates indigenous peoples who are still here. This museum is not about dead Indians; it is the embodiment of living traditions, but traditions now threatened throughout the Americas and around the world as a result of global burning.

LIFE-ENHANCING CULTURES OF HOMELAND MATURITY

As new ways to thrive in life-enhancing cultures are sought out, indigenous traditions and worldviews must be acknowledged. Many scientists now recognize the knowledges of indigenous peoples. Groups like the American Indian and Alaska Native Climate Change Working Group are encouraging indigenous students to play to their strengths as indigenous holistic thinkers and enter scientific fields. Tribal colleges and universities are working to ensure that our indigenous tribal knowledge of landscapes and climates are valued and incorporated into geosciences education and research. Oren Lyons, Faithkeeper of the

Turtle clan of the Onondaga Nation, and many of our elders remind us that if we see the natural world as full of relatives, not resources, good things will happen.

American Indian and Alaska Native wisdom is a cooperative construction built on generations of attentive interaction between humans and the diversity of life found in the unique ecosystems and environments we call home. How will we protect our homes and homelands?

Unlike the military-industrial system of homeland security many now seek, indigenous traditions suggest the development of an urgently needed experience-based *homeland maturity*: life-enhancing knowledges emergent from experience in the rich contours of the nature-culture nexus, a maturity that shows we respect our Mother Earth and the rich diversity of life that we humans are one small, but important, part of. We have reached a place and time where hopefully humankind will acknowledge that we cannot expect much security on this beautiful blue-green planet until we, humankind, demonstrate some much needed homeland maturity.

ENDNOTES

INTRODUCTION

1. http://climatecongress.ku.dk/speakers/keymessagesandsummary .ppt/.
2. Planning for Seven Generations: Indigenous and Scientific Approaches to Climate Change, www.cbp.ucar.edu/tribalagenda. html.

CHAPTER ONE

1. Billy Frank Jr., "Where Do We Go from Here? The Legacies of Vine Deloria Jr.," symposium, University of Arizona, November 10, 2006.

CHAPTER TWO

1. www4.nau.edu/tribalclimatechange/tribes/docs/tribes_Respecting TEK.ppt.
2. Tecumseh, "Indians Must Unite to Fight against the Americans," http://eolit.hrw.com/hlla/rw/index2.jsp?Chapter=61&Page=1.
3. Robert K. Thomas, "The Taproots of Peoplehood," *Americans Before Columbus* 10, no. 5 (Albuquerque, NM: National Indian Youth Council), 1982.
4. Vine Deloria Jr., *Power and Place: Indian Education in America* (Golden, CO: Fulcrum, 2001).

CHAPTER THREE

1. www4.nau.edu/tribalclimatechange/tribes/docs/tribes_Respecting TEK.ppt.

CHAPTER FOUR

1. Dan Vergano, "Global Carbon Levels Spiraling," *USA Today*, May 22, 2007, www.usatoday.com/news/world/2007-05-21-carbon-levels_N .htm?csp=34&loc=interstitialskip.
2. John Waggoner, "Investors Fish for Profit in Clean Water," USA Today, May 23, 2007, www.usatoday.com/money/perfi/funds/2007-05-23-water-funds_N.htm.
3. International Union for Conservation of Nature Red List, "Release of the 2006 IUCN Red List of Threatened Species Reveals Ongoing Decline of the Status of Plants and Animals," May 4, 2006, www .flmnh.ufl.edu/fish/organizations/ssg/2006Mayredlist.pdf.
4. Planning for Seven Generations, Indigenous and Scientific Approaches to Climate Change, www.cbp.ucar.edu/tribalagenda.html.

CHAPTER FIVE

1. www.waterhistory.org/histories/hohokam2/hohokam2.pdf.
2. David R. Wilcox, Phil C. Wiegand, J. Scott Wood, and Jerry B. Howard, "Ancient Cultural Interplay of the American Southwest in the Mexican Northwest," *Journal of the Southwest*, June 22, 2008.
3. *Menominee Tribal Enterprises: The Menominee Forest-Based Sustainable Development Tradition,* Maeqtekuahkihkiw Kew Kanāhwihtahquaq, "The Forest Keepers," 1997, http://epa.gov/ ecopage/upland/menominee/forestkeepers.pdf.
4. Thomas Davis, *Sustaining the Forest, the People, and the Spirit* (Albany, NY: SUNY, 2000), 4.
5. *Menominee Tribal Enterprises.*
6. Ronald L. Trosper, "Indigenous Influence on Forest Management on the Menominee Indian Reservation," *Forest Ecology and Management*, 249, nos. 1–2 (September 25, 2007): 134–139.
7. www.windpoweringamerica.gov/filter_detail.asp?itemid=677.

CHAPTER SIX

1. www.ncdc.noaa.gov/oa/climate/research/2006/jul.
2. www.ncdc.noaa.gov/oa/climate/research/2006/jul/julyext2006.html.

CHAPTER SEVEN

1. Deborah Epstein Popper and Frank J. Popper, "The Great Plains: From Dust to Dust," *Planning* (December 1987).
2. Kristen Bibbins-Domingo, Pamela Coxson, Mark J. Pletcher, James Lightwood, and Lee Goldman, "Adolescent Overweight and Future Adult Coronary Heart Disease," *The New England Journal of Medicine* 357, no. 23 (December 6, 2007): 2371–2379.

SPEAKER'S CORNER is a provocative series designed to stimulate, educate, and foster discussion on significant topics facing society. Written by experts in a variety of fields, these engaging books should be read by anyone interested in the trends and issues that shape our world.

For a complete list of all titles in the Speaker's Corner series, please contact us at:

 FULCRUM PUBLISHING

3970 Youngfield Street
Wheat Ridge, CO 80033
E-mail: info@fulcrumbooks.com
Toll-free: 800-992-2908
Fax: 800-726-7112
fulcrumbooks.com